# a VISION *of* HOPE

## *for the* END

# TIMES

## WHY I WANT TO
## BE LEFT BEHIND

## R. LOREN SANDFORD

DESTINY IMAGE® PUBLISHERS, INC.
P.O. Box 310, Shippensburg, PA 17257-0310
*Promoting Inspired Lives.*

This book and all other Destiny Image and Destiny Image Fiction books are available at Christian bookstores and distributors worldwide.

Cover design by: Eileen Rockwell
Interior design by Terry Clifton

For more information on foreign distributors, call 717-532-3040.
Reach us on the Internet: www.destinyimage.com.

ISBN 13 TP: 978-0-7684-4566-4
ISBN 13 eBook: 978-0-7684-4567-1
ISBN 13 HC: 978-0-7684-4569-5
ISBN 13 LP: 978-0-7684-4568-8

For Worldwide Distribution, Printed in the U.S.A.
1 2 3 4 5 6 7 8 / 22 21 20 19 18

# DEDICATION

EVERY FATHER OF A SON—IF HE IS A REAL FATHER— dreams that his son will one day stand beside him as a man and even grow beyond him. Jesus Himself, speaking from the heart of Father God, said that we who believe would do greater works than He did. I have such a son. Much of my thinking that inspired this book was sparked by challenges he issued in our joint labor pastoring New Song Church and Ministries together in Denver, Colorado. I therefore dedicate this book to Nathaniel Loren Sandford, my beloved son.

# CONTENTS

# INTRODUCTION

EVER SINCE THE FOUNDING OF THE CURRENT NATION-state of Israel in 1948, the body of Christ has seen a virtual frenzy of end-time speculation. In the ensuing years, for instance, considerable effort has been expended in failed attempts to make current events in the Middle East fit a supposed biblical timeline based on the establishment of the state of Israel.

Books have come and gone over the years, setting dates for the return of Jesus, or at least establishing expectations of His return within a certain time frame. Some of us remember reading books claiming that Jesus would return within thirty-five years of the founding of Israel—a supposed biblical generation. When this didn't materialize, some writers and preachers adjusted the definition of a biblical generation to forty years, and I have even caught wind of some who moved it out to seventy years. I call that "rubber prophecy"—stretch-to-fit! It didn't work and it never will. "Truly I say to you, this generation will not pass away until all these things take place" (Mark 13:30). Clearly, Jesus meant the actual people standing before Him, not a generation of people alive nearly 2,000 years later.

I'm old enough to recall the pseudo-scholarly books and prophecies published in the early to mid-seventies declaring the European Union to be the revived ten-nation end-time Roman Empire that people believed the Revelation to John prophesied. At this writing, the European Union has grown to twenty-seven member states after the departure of Great Britain. So much for that one!

Then came a flood of speculation concerning the identity of the antichrist. At one point, if memory serves, some claimed it was former Secretary of State Henry Kissinger. I recall one book from the 1970s—title forgotten—that pointed to the Prince of

Spain. Some now claim it's the rise of Islam. This has led to speculation about the mark of the beast and fear-mongering over microchips embedded in people's hands that are supposed to be that mark.

Books containing this kind of content have sold hundreds of thousands of copies, while little or none of what has been written has ever actually unfolded. Multitudes of innocent and hopeful believers have been set up for disappointment in a frenzy of unjustified excitement. Predictions of wars, who would be involved in them, the return of Jesus, and many other confident prognostications have never truly materialized. Some of it has been clearly ludicrous. For instance, I recall attending weekend concerts at Calvary Chapel in Costa Mesa, California at the height of the Jesus Movement where people outside the building were passing out pamphlets claiming that the Russians were building tanks of compressed wood so that the smoke of their burning could rise to heaven in fulfillment of the prophecy in Revelation. Such foolishness we have seen over the years!

Added together, all this seems to be a huge confusing ball of tangled twine. At best, most of us—rightly, I hope—expect the return of the Lord in our lifetime. At worst, we make ourselves appear to outsiders as a bunch of fools willing to believe anything we're told, no matter how ridiculous it may seem, regardless of how poorly undergirded with rational thought and solid scholarship it might be.

In all this unfounded excitement over supposed signs and portents that never really result in anything, I suggest that we ought to be more obsessed with the kingdom of God manifest on earth among us in power and victory than with the rapture and the end of days. Why be obsessed with escape when we should be walking in victory and impacting the world in which we now live?

It is my hope that this book can undo a few of the more common misunderstandings current in the body of Christ and restore a measure of sanity to an increasingly confused field of speculation and biblical distortion. I know that what I write will raise more questions than I have pages available to answer. I'm also certain that I don't have all the answers, nor does anyone I know. Apparently, God leaves us with some mysteries that will not be explained until Jesus actually returns.

This book includes summaries of opposing positions on the subject of the end times that I will have neither space nor patience to fully address, even as I may refer to them. I'm certain that in the process I will offend a great many people and have braced myself to endure a drenching in the blood of a virtual herd of sacred cows. I do, however, bear the strongest commitment to the truth of the Word of God and to responsible scholarship rooted in the historic, cultural, linguistic, and textual contexts that together determine the meaning of any passage or prophecy of Scripture.

While I have taken care to solidly root everything I have written here in the infallible Word of God, the Bible, I have also laced this book with prophetic foresights of what I believe will be taking place. I believe these things are consonant with the Scriptures, but they provide a bit more than simple interpretation of the Word.

None of the issues I raise touch on conditions for salvation or any core doctrine of our faith, nor do they constitute reasons for division among believers. Anyone who has surrendered his or her life to Jesus the Son of God—the second Person of the Trinity, the one true God, born of a virgin, who died in my place as a sacrifice for my sin and rose again from the dead—is my brother or sister. We must stand together in love. We can disagree on issues of prophecies of the end times, but not on these core definitions of the nature of God and our salvation.

Now bear with me for a few pages as we establish some foundational understandings before the fun really begins! If you find this first chapter too scholarly, more than you really want to know, skip to the next one.

# CHAPTER 1

# DEFINITIONS OF ESSENTIAL TERMS

Fɪʀsᴛ, ʏᴏᴜ ᴡɪʟʟ ᴇɴᴄᴏᴜɴᴛᴇʀ ᴛʜᴇ ᴡᴏʀᴅ *ESCHATOLOGY* several times in reading this book. Simply defined, it means "the study of the end times." Second, much of the confusion I've described in the introduction stems from failure to understand the differences between biblical genres. Christians tend to lump prophetic writings together with apocalyptic literature and call it all "prophecy," but the differences between prophecy and apocalyptic literature are profound. A good grasp of these differences goes a long way toward comprehending what the writers were actually trying to tell us.

## Pʀᴏᴘʜᴇᴄʏ ᴠᴇʀsᴜs Aᴘᴏᴄᴀʟʏᴘᴛɪᴄ

### Definitions

**Prophecy:** The root New Testament Greek word is *prophemi. Pro* means "forth" while *phemi* means "to speak." At its core, prophecy is simply speaking forth God's word. We have tended to define it too narrowly as predicting the future, but this doesn't fit the full biblical definition. See, for instance, Isaiah, Jeremiah, and Ezekiel, as well as the minor prophets. The focus of their ministries was to deliver the word of God to call Israel back from idolatry in order cleanse its influence from their lives, their culture, and the practice of their faith. Prediction of coming events received a much a lesser emphasis and was most often, though not always, conditional upon Israel's choice whether or not to repent and mend their ways.

**Apocalyptic:** The word comes from the Greek *apokalupsis. Apo* means "from" and *kalupsis* means "veil," "hidden." Put them together and the word means "revelation of what is hidden, disclosure or uncovering." Parts of Daniel can be classified

9

as apocalyptic literature while nearly the entire Book of Revelation falls into that genre.

Prophecy is not apocalyptic and apocalyptic is not prophecy.

### Contrast #1

*Prophecy* in the Old Testament began as spoken words written down by observers or by disciples and scribes who accompanied the prophets. In short, prophecy is spoken.

*Apocalyptic* began as literature, meaning that it was written, as opposed to being spoken. From the very beginning it was printed material, as opposed to transcription of the spoken words of a recognized prophet.

### Contrast #2

The language of *prophecy* is direct and simple in style, needing very little interpretation. The prophets often employed metaphorical language to liken Israel, for instance, to an adulterous wife or to a son who has forgotten his father, but they shied away from symbolism whose meaning might not be immediately clear to those listening.

By contrast, *apocalyptic* deliberately conceals the intended message by expressing it in wild symbolism presented as dreams and visions needing interpretation. In other words, apocalyptic authors wrote in a code that only their intended audiences could decipher, having been schooled in the code. In taking this approach, they sought to attract as little attention as possible from enemies, real and potential, by concealing the identities of the people and nations concerning whom they wrote.

## Contrast #3

In *prophecy*, in cases where prediction actually forms a part of the prophetic word, the emphasis falls on the present casting light on the future. We might view it as prophecy with prediction. Certain blessings and restorations will happen, for instance, if the people repent. Isaiah 58 stands as a classic example. God promised to restore Israel's blessing if they would repent of violating the Sabbath and begin ministering to the poor and homeless. In other places, the prophets predict the destruction of Israel that must come as the direct result of their continued disobedience and failure to repent. In prophecy, the present determines the future, and is most often conditional upon how God's people choose to respond to the prophetic word.

In *apocalyptic*, the future casts light on the present to provide both hope and certainty in uncertain times. It is prediction with prophecy, as opposed to prophecy with prediction, as you will see in a moment.

In *prophecy*, therefore, repentance is key. The future can be altered depending on whether or not God's people respond to the call. Prophecy focuses on the behavior of God's people and the purity of their devotion. It presents a future most often determined by a set of "ifs" and "thens."

By contrast, in *apocalyptic* the future has been set in stone by a sovereign God and cannot be changed. God has determined the end from the beginning. Apocalyptic came into being as "tracts for hard times," intended for seasons when God's people lived under threat of persecution, trial, and uncertainty. Rather than focus on a call for repentance, apocalyptic literature presents God's unchanging promises to the faithful. It speaks to and/or interprets the present in light of a certain future.

The unrighteous who persecute the people of God will be judged, while the righteous will be gathered into glory. The current period of trial and trouble therefore constitutes only a temporary season. Thus, the future makes sense of the present to inject hope and certainty into uncertain times.

### The Message

In *prophecy,* the message is for the "now" with the hope of producing a righteous nation summoned out of idolatry and immorality to return to a complete dedication to the Lord alone. Prophecy seeks to heal a broken nation.

*Apocalyptic* literature assumes the existence of a righteous remnant and promises vindication for them in the last days. It looks forward to the decisive and final destruction of evil and assures the righteous of the coming of the heavenly kingdom.

# SUMMARY

Both spoken prophecy and apocalyptic literature present history as a constant revelation of God's purposes for the world (see Jer. 18:1-12 and 23:5-8). **Prophecy** presents this in terms of ongoing salvation and the relationship between God and His people. **Apocalyptic** speaks in terms of the final consummation of history in glory, the revelation of God's sovereignty, and the vindication of the saints (see Dan. 7:23-28 and Rev. 7:13-17).

# OTHER DEFINITIONS

### The Great Tribulation

The biblical Greek word for "tribulation" is *thlipsis,* meaning "affliction, oppression, or harassment." Generally, the Great Tribulation is understood as a seven-year period of intense trouble and suffering on earth, literal or symbolic in duration, immediately preceding the return of the Lord. Teachers differ on this next point but, in my view, the Great Tribulation in Scripture includes the persecution of Christians who remain on the earth throughout.

Much of the suffering brought upon mankind as a whole during this period of time, as well as the persecution of Christians, is usually attributed to the activity of Satan. It is as though Satan, knowing that he has but a limited time, seeks to inflict as much damage as he can before the Lord returns to put an end to his reign and influence. On the other hand, many commentators interpret this period of time as God's judgment upon the world.

## The Rapture

The rapture refers to the catching up of the saints to meet the Lord in the air at His return. The English word derives from the Latin *rapturo* rather than the original Greek of the Bible. In Greek, the word is the verb *harpazo* (see 1 Thess. 4:17), meaning "caught up." Christians tend to argue violently over the question of whether the catching up of the saints happens before, during, or after the Great Tribulation, although scholars and teachers increasingly lean toward a post-tribulation position.

## The Millennium

Generally speaking, this refers to the thousand-year reign of Christ on earth. Three different views of the millennium are held within the pale of orthodoxy. In other words, it is entirely possible to hold any one of these three views without departing from the central and essential tenets of our faith. This means that we should be able to discuss the issue rationally and lovingly, although entire denominations have been formed from church splits rooted in disputes over how to view the millennium. Some feel the 1,000-year number is literal while others believe it to be symbolic. The following definitions are somewhat over-simplified, but useful for the average reader.

*Postmillennialism* holds that Jesus will return at the end of a thousand-year period during which the saints have established the kingdom of God on earth. *Premillennialism* posits that Jesus will return to end the present age and *begin* a literal thousand-year reign upon earth. As the name of a position, *amillenialism* sounds a bit misleading because it seems as though amillennialists deny the idea of any thousand-year reign of Christ at all. In short, rather than reject the idea of the millennium altogether, amillennialism most often sees symbolism in the millennial prophecies, denying only a literal thousand-year reign. Many amillennialists believe that the millennium symbolically represents the coming of the kingdom of God to earth in power in and through the gift of the Spirit on the day of Pentecost.

# CHAPTER 2

# THE PARADOX AND PROMISE OF THE AGE

A LL OVER THE INTERNET AND IN BOOKS I HAVE READ, I hear and see Christians feeding on fear because they see the world descending into a state of turmoil and disintegration. As a result, they believe the end times are upon us, or nearly so. As far as the idea that the end times are nearly upon us, I have no substantive disagreement. Listening to this fear, however, you'd think we're all powerless, that we're losing the battle, and that Jesus must therefore return to set everything straight at the point of our defeat. It's as though we must therefore brace ourselves because things are going to get worse and in the midst of it we're all helpless victims until Jesus returns.

Some folks believe that Jesus will return before all the worst trouble unfolds, that He will then rapture the church out of the world and up to heaven, leaving the earth to a seven-year period of destruction. Others of us firmly believe that things will indeed get worse, but that the Great Tribulation will unfold while we remain to stand in the midst of it, and *then* Jesus will come to catch us up to Himself in the rapture. Thus is born the pre-tribulation/post-tribulation rapture debate.

No matter which position you take, the problem in this is that in the face of all it, most Christians seem to adopt some form of defeatist attitude and belief. At heart, they believe the world is going to hell in a handbasket and there's nothing we can do about it except wait for Jesus to come back to rescue us, fearful in the meantime of what might happen to us.

Others believe that we'll establish the kingdom here on earth as we take control of each of the seven mountains of influence for Jesus—religion, arts and entertainment, media, education, government, business, and family. In other words, we'll establish a literal kingdom of God here by Spirit-empowered human effort, and when Jesus returns we'll deliver it up to Him, ready and prepared for Him to assume the throne. We call this Dominionism, but the problem is that it doesn't line up with Scripture, and especially not with Jesus's own words in Matthew 24. To be fair to the Dominionists, the truth in what they teach is that we must infiltrate and influence every segment of society, each of those seven mountains, transforming the atmosphere around us and winning souls by our demonstration of the Father's heart, the Word of God, and the power of the kingdom of God. That being said, where does the reality lie concerning the last days?

## ISAIAH'S PROPHECY

The truth begins with a wonderfully simple affirmation. *No matter how it plays out, we get to win.*

> *Arise, shine; for your light has come, and the glory of the Lord has risen upon you. For behold, darkness will cover the earth and deep darkness the peoples; but the Lord will rise upon you and His glory will appear upon you. Nations will come to your light, and kings to the brightness of your rising. Lift up your eyes round about and see; they all gather together, they come to you. Your sons will come from afar, and your daughters will be carried in the arms* (Isaiah 60:1-4).

In context, Isaiah prophesied concerning the restoration of Israel to the land after the exile to Babylon that began in 586 B.C. when Nebuchadnezzar's armies destroyed Israel and Jerusalem. The Babylonian exile lasted seventy years, after which the people did, in fact, return to rebuild their shattered capital city and their nation, but the fullness of what Isaiah foresaw in these verses never actually came to pass historically. For literal Israel, the level of glory presented in Isaiah never truly unfolded.

The verses that follow these speak of prosperity for Israel and enormous numerical increase. Isaiah's vision of the future also included foreigners building up Israel's walls and the nations of the world bringing them wealth, favor, and honor at a level that literal Israel never experienced. In fact, much of what Isaiah prophesied could be truly fulfilled only later, in Jesus, as people from every tribe, tongue, and nation have turned to Israel's true Messiah.

As is the case with many prophets, Isaiah spoke from "prophetic perspective." In other words, he saw events covering more than one period of time layered into a single picture, as if each of the pictures were Photoshopped so that every layer could be seen simultaneously with varying degrees of opacity. In that light, we can see that some of what Isaiah saw applied to what happened in the fifth and sixth centuries B.C., while more was blended into a vision that would not be fulfilled for centuries yet to come.

> *No longer will you have the sun for light by day, nor for brightness will the moon give you light; but you will have the Lord for an everlasting light, and your God for your glory. Your sun will no longer set, nor will your moon wane; for you will have the Lord for an everlasting light, and the days of your mourning will be over* (Isaiah 60:19-20).

Obviously, these things did not occur in the years following the exile or at any other time in Israel's history. Who, then, is our everlasting light and how has this word been fulfilled? Answer: Only in Jesus.

> *Then all your people will be righteous; they will possess the land forever, the branch of My planting, the work of My hands, that I may be glorified. The smallest one will become a clan, and the least one a mighty nation. I, the Lord, will hasten it in its time* (Isaiah 60:21-22).

Only in Jesus, by His sacrifice of His own body on the cross, could all the people of God be made righteous, covered with His goodness imputed to us. He cleansed us and made us holy by His sacrifice for sin. Since then, in Him the number of God's people has grown to such an extent that they cannot even be counted. These promises were never truly realized in the history of literal Israel.

# THE PROMISE

The pieces of Isaiah's prophecy that found no fulfillment in literal Israel must be viewed as a last days promise applicable to spiritual Israel, both Jews and Gentiles who have received the King of Kings. These verses convey a message of hope and resounding victory for believers in a darkening age much like ours. In doing so, the promise presents us with two elements that appear to be contradictory—a paradox.

First, *deep darkness covers the nations.* As dangers increase and society deteriorates, the world situation will appear to be growing worse. Scripture—especially Matthew 24 with its prophecies of lovelessness, lawlessness, persecution of believers, famines, wars, and rumors of wars—cannot be denied.

Second, at the same time Isaiah paints a picture in which *God's chosen ones walk in glorious favor.* People from every tribe, tongue, and nation come to know the Lord, join the company of God's people, and bring their wealth with them. Why? Because of the bright shining of the Lord's favor upon us, His people. "Nations will come to your light, and kings to the brightness of your rising" (Isa. 60:3). In many parts of the world, such a move of God is now under way.

We get to win. Does this mean that we take over the world, the seven mountains, and establish a literal government on earth prior to the return of the Lord? Not according to Isaiah and other passages of Scripture. Does this mean that we affect multitudes from every nation, lead them to the light, and change the very atmosphere around us just by being who we are in the Lord? A resounding *yes!* Does it mean that we will penetrate every nation on earth and lead people to Jesus for their lives to be transformed? Yes.

Even now we see a cultural shift in response to the ministry of the Father's heart through believers bold enough to reach out. While laws and court cases come against us and the radical left hurls hate and accusation, openness to the ministry of the Spirit on the part of unbelievers has never been greater, at least not in my lifetime. Where once an offer of prayer for a hurting person in the world outside the walls of the church would be met with firm rejection, there is now a hungry, positive response: "Oh yes! Thank you!" Love wins. Light conquers darkness. Hearts are opening.

# MATTHEW 24 IN PROPHETIC PERSPECTIVE

### Notes on Sorting Out Prophetic Perspective

In sorting out prophetic perspective to determine what has already come to pass versus what must yet transpire, three questions must be asked. 1) Was this prophecy fulfilled one to one in history? If there is no foreshadowing of something greater to come and no unfulfilled elements included in the prophecy, then we should expect nothing more in the future. 2) Was there a fulfillment in history, but not in the fullness of what was prophesied? For instance, in Acts 2 Peter declared that the outpouring of the Spirit on the day of Pentecost fulfilled Joel 2:28, but a comparison of the passages reveals that not everything Joel prophesied happened at Pentecost. Something greater is foreshadowed. While we recognize the truth of what Peter spoke that day, we nevertheless expect a later outpouring that fulfills all the elements of what Joel foresaw. 3) Has any fulfillment at all been seen in history? If not, then we expect something yet to come.

Now we apply this to the words of Jesus.

### Matthew 24

> *Jesus came out from the temple and was going away when His disciples came up to point out the temple buildings to Him. And He said to them, "Do you not see all these things? Truly I say to you, not one stone here will be left upon another, which will not be torn down"* (Matthew 24:1-2).

This unfolded in A.D. 70 when Rome brutally crushed the Jewish revolt that began in A.D. 66. In the following verses, we see a shift in the content of Jesus's words as prophetic perspective shows us prophecies that apply to multiple periods of time all layered onto one image.

*As He was sitting on the Mount of Olives, the disciples came to Him privately, saying, "Tell us, when will these things happen, and what will be the sign of Your coming, and of the end of the age?" And Jesus answered and said to them, "See to it that no one misleads you. For many will come in My name, saying, 'I am the Christ,' and will mislead many. You will be hearing of wars and rumors of wars. See that you are not frightened, for those things must take place, but that is not yet the end. For nation will rise against nation, and kingdom against kingdom, and in various places there will be famines and earthquakes. But all these things are merely the beginning of birth pangs. Then they will deliver you to tribulation, and will kill you, and you will be hated by all nations because of My name. At that time many will fall away and will betray one another and hate one another. Many false prophets will arise and will mislead many. Because lawlessness is increased, most people's love will grow cold. But the one who endures to the end, he will be saved. This gospel of the kingdom shall be preached in the whole world as a testimony to all the nations, and then the end will come"* (Matthew 24:3-14).

Jesus presented the disciples with two realities applicable to the last days. First, yes, wars and rumors of wars will increase, as will famines, earthquakes, and natural disasters. Yes, there will be false christs. Menachem, the messianic pretender involved in the Jewish revolt against Roman rule in A.D. 66, was such a one. So was Bar Kochba who led the second Jewish revolt in A.D. 135. Both rebellions failed disastrously. The first disaster unfolded in fulfillment of Jesus's prophecy that every stone in the temple would be torn down. In the centuries since then, more messianic claimants have arisen. Some pretenders make that claim today. Where wars and rumors of wars are concerned, the world seems a boiling pot of conflict in our own time.

Yes, it will be a season when hatred against Christians increases and many fall away, just as it was in the years following Pentecost, and just as we see in the world today when there have been more believers martyred for their faith in the last couple of decades than in the entire prior history of the church combined. Yes, it will be a time when most people's love grows cold. Again, we see this in our time as the spirit of hatred grows, spreads, and results in acts of violence based in racism, ethnic conflict, religious persecution, domestic violence, marital breakups, and senseless acts of murder. Marriages fail at record rates, families break up, and young men, lost and angry, shoot up schools. The culture of self captivates the multitudes at the expense of love for fellow man, while the spirit of offense permeates society. None of this can be avoided or denied.

Second, at the same time that all of this trouble increases, the crescendo of our victory will grow, just as it did in the first century. An unprecedented outpouring of God's Spirit will be released in a flood of glory and hope, the like of which we've never seen or known. Even now it begins, just as it unfolded so long ago for those gathered on the day of Pentecost in the Upper Room.

We will see a great ingathering of souls coming to Jesus through us, seeking relief from the suffering sin produces. In many corners of the world this has already begun. They will come because the love of most in the world around us will have grown cold—and already has—and because the Father God shines His power and love through us for healing and restoration. As Isaiah said, "Lift up your eyes round about and see; they all gather together, they come to you." Lonely and hurting people will seek places of refuge and healing and they will find them in us.

Then follows the part of Matthew 24 that too many miss when prognosticating about end-time events: "This gospel of the kingdom shall be preached in the whole world as a testimony to all the nations, and then the end will come" (Matt. 24:14). Jesus's prophecy in Matthew 24 finds confirmation in Revelation 7:9: "After these things I looked, and behold, a great multitude which no one could count, from every nation and all tribes and peoples and tongues, standing before the throne and before the Lamb, clothed in white robes, and palm branches were in their hands." When every people group on earth has had opportunity to hear and respond to the gospel, the end will come.

Clearly, we must expect a great victorious harvest of souls from every ethnic group around the world, an ingathering so huge that the numbers cannot be counted. In keeping with this ingathering, the palm branches in Revelation 7:9 point to a victory celebration. I therefore say it again: We get to win. Any theology that feeds on defeat and loss leading to Jesus's return must be rejected. We've been given a gospel of victory, not of defeat and loss.

Joel 2:28 speaks of a fresh outpouring of the Holy Spirit on all flesh in the last days that will include dreams, visions, and people calling on the Lord. By anyone's measure, this means that Joel foresaw a time of decisive victory and blessing for the people of God before the end. In Acts 2, Peter called the outpouring on the day of Pentecost the fulfillment of Joel's prophecy, but there was more in the context of that prophecy than actually occurred at Pentecost. Again, prophetic perspective is in play. There is more to come that will completely fulfill the Lord's Word and fill out the picture of our triumph.

## THE GREAT PRE-TRIBULATION RAPTURE DECEPTION

Jesus Himself described the events that will accompany and validate the reality of His return:

> *For the coming of the Son of Man will be just like the days of Noah. For as in those days before the flood they were eating and drinking, marrying and giving in marriage, until the day that Noah entered the ark, and they did not understand until the flood came and took them all away; so will the coming of the Son of Man be* (Matthew 24:37-39).

This passage has frequently been misinterpreted to support pre-tribulation rapture theory, the idea that the saints will be taken off the earth to be rescued while sinners remain behind to suffer seven years of trouble. If the key words, however, are "just like," then who did God remove from the earth when the flood came? Answer: the wicked, not the righteous. Who remained to inherit the earth? Answer: Noah and his family. The flood took the wicked away and left righteous Noah and his family to possess and repopulate the earth. The first "rapture" that took people off the earth took the wicked out from among the righteous by means of the waters of the flood while Noah remained. Jesus said that it will be just like that at the end. The wicked will be taken out first and we win!

> Then there will be two men in the field; one will be taken and one will be left. Two women will be grinding at the mill; one will be taken and one will be left. Therefore be on the alert, for you do not know which day your Lord is coming. But be sure of this, that if the head of the house had known at what time of the night the thief was coming, he would have been on the alert and would not have allowed his house to be broken into. For this reason you also must be ready; for the Son of Man is coming at an hour when you do not think He will. Who then is the faithful and sensible slave whom his master put in charge of his household to give them their food at the proper time? Blessed is that slave whom his master finds so doing when he comes. Truly I say to you that he will put him in charge of all his possessions (Matthew 24:40-47).

Focus on that last line. When Jesus returns, the wicked will be taken out and the righteous on earth will be put in charge of all that belongs to God. Jesus never presented a scenario in which God removes the church and abandons the earth to its destruction. We win. While we cannot therefore deny or discount Jesus's own prophecy that the troubles outlined in Matthew 24 will come in the form of earthquakes, wars, pestilence, famines, false christs, and persecution of believers, we must not go looking for, dwelling on, and being afraid of every conspiracy theory that comes around. Too many of us have camped on the craziness and the negatives as if these were the whole story. They're not. Jesus Himself said:

> *But immediately after the tribulation of those days the sun will be darkened, and the moon will not give its light, and the stars will fall from the sky, and the powers of the heavens will be shaken. And then the sign of the Son of Man will appear in the sky, and then all the tribes of the earth will mourn, and they will see the Son of Man coming on the clouds of the sky with power and great glory. And He will send forth His angels with a great trumpet and they will gather together His elect from the four winds, from one end of the sky to the other* (Matthew 24:29-31).

In the late 1960s and early '70s when a whole generation of Jesus People bought into the idea of a pre-tribulation rapture, what part of "after" did we not understand? *After* the Great Tribulation, not before, He will gather His chosen ones as He comes on the clouds of heaven. In fact, He made it very clear that we must not believe that He has returned in any form or manner unless the whole world sees Him on the clouds of heaven.

*Then if anyone says to you, "Behold, here is the Christ," or "There He is," do not believe him. For false Christs and false prophets will arise and will show great signs and wonders, so as to mislead, if possible, even the elect. Behold, I have told you in advance. So if they say to you, "Behold, He is in the wilderness," do not go out, or, "Behold, He is in the inner rooms," do not believe them. For just as the lightning comes from the east and flashes even to the west, so will the coming of the Son of Man be* (Matthew 24:23-27).

All will see Him in a very public way, just as all see flashes of lightning during a thunderstorm. Could it be any clearer? Pre-tribulation rapture theory requires that there be two comings of Jesus, the first one secret and the second seen by the whole world. In Matthew 24, Jesus made it obvious that we must not believe in any claim that the Lord has returned, or will return, except in a manner that the entire world will see. This will not be the moment of our escape, but rather our victory celebration.

We must therefore view all this very differently than we have traditionally. Jesus will come at a time we don't expect, not to take the saints away to abandon the earth to its fate with the wicked in charge, but first to take out the wicked from among the righteous. We must be found faithfully taking care of the kingdom of God when that happens, and we must do it with a positive kingdom attitude of heart.

Is there a rapture of the saints when we're caught up to meet Him? Absolutely! Right now, however, I'm saying that God has destined us to be in charge of all that is His—the household of this earth. Entrusted with the things of God, we will ultimately receive authority over a redeemed planet. "But according to His promise we are looking for new heavens and a new earth, in which righteousness dwells" (2 Pet. 3:13).

If deep darkness covers the peoples, and if a time of trouble does, in fact, precede the Lord's return as He Himself told us, then more of what Isaiah prophesied is also true:

> *The Lord will rise upon you and His glory will appear upon you. Nations will come to your light, and kings to the brightness of your rising. Lift up your eyes round about and see; they all gather together, they come to you. Your sons will come from afar, and your daughters will be carried in the arms* (Isaiah 60:2-4).

As a result, when all of this unfolds and proceeds to its conclusion, we followers of Christ will be put in charge. We inherit ultimate authority over the earth.

## The Parables of the Kingdom

Matthew 24 wasn't the first time Jesus taught that the unrighteous constitute the first harvest out of the earth. The same message is recorded in Matthew 13:

> *Jesus presented another parable to them, saying, "The kingdom of heaven may be compared to a man who sowed good seed in his field. But while his men were sleeping, his enemy came and sowed tares among the wheat, and went away. But when the wheat sprouted and bore grain, then the tares*

*became evident also. The slaves of the landowner came and said to him, 'Sir, did you not sow good seed in your field? How then does it have tares?' And he said to them, 'An enemy has done this!' The slaves said to him, 'Do you want us, then, to go and gather them up?' But he said, 'No; for while you are gathering up the tares, you may uproot the wheat with them. Allow both to grow together until the harvest; and in the time of the harvest I will say to the reapers, "First gather up the tares and bind them in bundles to burn them up; but gather the wheat into my barn"'"* (Matthew 13:24-30).

*First*, gather up the tares, the weeds, the wicked, *then* the righteous. Jesus never taught the first ingathering as the rapture in which we all escape and leave the earth to the wicked. That's escapist defeatism. Clearly, the first gathering out of the earth will remove not the righteous, but the wicked destined for destruction. *Then* He gathers us who believe into His waiting arms. We win. With Him we inherit the earth.

Jesus's own interpretation of the parable follows.

*Then He left the crowds and went into the house. And His disciples came to Him and said, "Explain to us the parable of the tares of the field." And He said, "The one who sows the good seed is the Son of Man, and the field is the world; and as for the good seed, these are the sons of the kingdom; and the tares are the sons of the evil one; and the enemy who sowed them is the devil, and the harvest is the end of the age; and the reapers are angels. So just*

31

*as the tares are gathered up and burned with fire,
so shall it be at the end of the age. The Son of Man
will send forth His angels, and they will gather out
of His kingdom all stumbling blocks, and those who
commit lawlessness, and will throw them into the
furnace of fire; in that place there will be weeping
and gnashing of teeth. Then the righteous will shine
forth as the sun in the kingdom of their Father. He
who has ears, let him hear"* (Matthew 13:36-43).

Clearly, the tares constitute the first harvest, rather than
the righteous who would then abandon the earth to the wicked
in their absence. When the Father gathers the wicked out of
His kingdom, the righteous inherit the earth. We who remain
then shine like the sun.

Jesus said it in the Sermon on the Mount: "Blessed are the
gentle, for they shall inherit the earth" (Matt. 5:5). We don't
abandon the earth. We rather inherit it. Nowhere do the Scriptures tell us that we lose the battle and then get rescued out of
the midst of defeat at the return of Jesus.

We must not therefore be found passively and anxiously
twiddling our thumbs, rejoicing that bad things are happening
in a darkening world, even while feeding on fear, thinking this
means that Jesus is coming soon and we get to escape. In truth,
this is the time of our rising, the time of our power and influence,
the season of our glory, even in the midst of gathering darkness.
Look again at Isaiah!

*For behold, darkness will cover the earth and deep
darkness the peoples; but the Lord will rise upon
you and His glory will appear upon you. Nations*

*will come to your light, and kings to the brightness of your rising. Lift up your eyes round about and see; they all gather together, they come to you. Your sons will come from afar, and your daughters will be carried in the arms* (Isaiah 60:2-4).

## STOP BEING FEARFUL

The last days present not a threat to the people of God, but a promise. Yet Christians far and wide seem to be captivated by every irresponsible fear-mongering conspiracy theory that comes along. Virtually none of such misguided pronouncements have any real basis in Scripture when examined in the light of the context in which they were written.

In order to understand the true message, we must study the *linguistic context*. The original documents were penned in Hebrew and Greek, not English or any other language. To fail to account for linguistic differences and language usage from thousands of years ago is to fail to understand the meaning of what the writers sought to convey.

We must account for the *historical context*, as well. Prophetic passages of Scripture weren't handed down in a vacuum. They spoke first to the historical settings and events in which they were delivered. This goes a long way toward helping us to sort out the layers of revelation embedded in prophetic perspective.

We must seek to comprehend the *cultural context* in which the prophets spoke and wrote. The culture of Bible times differed greatly from the culture of the twenty-first century. Reading the Word through the filter of a twenty-first century lens leads to all kinds of false conclusions.

Finally, we must study the *textual context*. What do the verses that come both before and after the passages we wish to study and understand actually say? In fact, what do the words themselves actually mean when left to speak for themselves?

In all of this, we must not impose some mystical interpretation of our own upon the text, but rather grasp the intended meaning of the author(s). Do this, and we will inevitably find that many contemporary fears dissipate in the light of the truth of who God really is and what He really intended us to understand.

## WHAT ABOUT ALL THAT BAD STUFF?

Some things are certainly true. False christs will emerge and, in fact, have already arisen, but Jesus said not to be frightened (see Matt. 24:6). There will be, and are, wars and rumors of wars. There will be, and are, famines and earthquakes in various places. All these seem to be increasing.

We must not fear these things. According to Matthew 24:8, events like these constitute the beginning of birth pangs as the whole of creation travails like a woman in childbirth to bring forth the age to come, the coming of the kingdom of God. I have three children of my own, as well as eleven wonderful grandchildren, and I know how frightening, and even painful, the birth of a child can be. The birth of a new baby, however, is also a time of joy and anticipation as we welcome something precious and wonderful into the world. Applying Jesus's metaphor, the same must be true of the birth of a new era of the kingdom of God on earth.

This season of both darkness and pain, therefore, abounds with hope, while the pain we read of in Scripture looks a lot like things trending in the age in which we currently live. As Isaiah stated, "darkness will cover the earth and deep darkness the peoples; but the Lord will rise upon you and His glory will appear upon you."

Christians will be, and are being, persecuted in increasing numbers. Hatred for believers grows and will continue to grow. All true! The devil hates us and seeks to enlist others in that hatred, but this is not a time for fear. It is rather the hour of our greatness!

Matthew 24:10 says, "many will fall away and will betray one another and hate one another." Also true and happening now! Society becomes ever more secular while in many segments of the church core doctrines are being cast aside. The spirit of hatred grows around the world. In my own nation, it manifests in racial division, racially motivated violence, and in an ever greater avalanche of vitriol between the left and the right, progressives and conservatives. This will be a time of false prophecy (see Matt. 24:11) as unfulfilled prophetic words and prognostications continue to proliferate.

Yes, lawlessness will increase and "most people's love will grow cold" (Matt. 24:12). Hatred now rises in the world and will continue to do so. And yet, "darkness will cover the earth and deep darkness the peoples; but the Lord will rise upon you and His glory will appear upon you." As servants of the Most High God, the time of the world's greatest trial becomes the hour of our greatest glory, power, and influence.

## THE VICTORY

Here's the most important element of our victory: "This gospel of the kingdom shall be preached in the whole world as a testimony to all the nations, and then the end will come" (Matt. 24:14). We don't lose. We win. Whether or not we disagree on the end-time significance of current events, one thing seems clear. When the gospel has been preached to every people group—*ethnos* (singular) or *ethnoi* (plural) in the Greek—then the end will come with the return of Jesus. According to every missiologist with whom I've spoken, the completion of that task is now in sight.

When souls from every walk of life, every "mountain of influence," are won to Jesus, Christian influence on society increases. People who have been changed by Jesus make changes in their spheres of influence. We change the atmosphere around us just by being who and what Jesus has made us to be.

## THE END-TIME OUTPOURING?

I see a new surge of the presence of God taking root around the world. As I write these words, a new Jesus Movement takes root among the young in my own church, and I hear similar reports from other sources. This time, however, the outpouring will include a fulfillment of Malachi 4:5-6, the hearts of the fathers restored to the children and the children to the fathers. Never again will there be a revival that affects a single generation. The "generation" who receive the last great outpouring will include people of every age. The Jesus Movement that flourished from approximately 1969 through the early 1970s was driven out of the existing churches by an older generation unable to receive it. The end-time revival won't be like that. Even though it may first catch fire among the young, and even though it will be their own unique expression, it will touch the whole people of God as one body.

The Jesus Movement died partly because its fathers abandoned their children, either unable to receive them into their churches or abandoning them when they fell into trouble and needed fathering the most. It can be argued that a young man named Lonnie Frisbee provided the spark that ignited the Jesus Movement, as well as the Vineyard movement that followed. Although I greatly respect the fathers of both Calvary Chapel where it all took flight and the Vineyard movement that carried it on, it must be said that when Lonnie began to experience serious moral trouble, his spiritual fathers weren't there for him. In the end, at least for a time, Lonnie was largely left out of the histories written about that great movement, his key role all but erased. In this last days outpouring, true spiritual fathers will not abandon their spiritual sons.

The generations differ in many ways because of the eras in which we grew up, but we stand united in the same Holy Spirit and the same passion. The dynamic of the Jesus Movement as it related to the older generation in the early 1970s was that the older generation under which I grew up didn't want the style and the look we younger ones brought with us. They wanted us to worship as they did, pray as they did, and dress as they did. Things have changed! It's a new day! Today, at least in circles where the Holy Spirit is welcomed to be Himself, the older generation longs for the young to be themselves in every way and feeds on their energy and freedom. This sets the stage for the fulfillment of Malachi's prophecy.

## THE PARADIGM SHIFT

I realize that, for many of us, the view of the end times I'm presenting constitutes a major paradigm shift, but hear me!

What I'm saying means that, regardless of whether Jesus returns soon or delays, my grandchildren have a future and a destiny. It gives all of us something to aspire to, a glorious destiny in hope and victory. We're not escaping and abandoning the earth to its destruction. We're winning.

Let me carry this a step farther. When we "boomers," born between the end of World War II and 1962, began to look to escape in an imminent rapture that would abandon the earth to its destruction, we unwittingly did so at the expense of the Lord's three-generational vision for the passing on of purpose and destiny to our descendants as articulated in Deuteronomy 6 and Acts 2. Consequently, we left our children without a vision or a hope, having failed to pass to them a consuming sense of destiny and purpose. This constitutes one of the many reasons the church has mostly lost an entire generation of young people.

We also paid a price in the solid grounding that education would have provided. Many young "Jesus freaks," as we were called, decided that because Jesus was returning so soon, they had no time to get an education. The imminent return of Jesus made evangelism so urgent that to spend four or more years in advanced study seemed foolish. Many of those have now faltered in faith as their hopes and dreams failed to materialize, while their lives and ministries—for those actually still ministering—remain limited for lack of training. Those of us, like me, who did pursue a solid education found ourselves equipped for the future and are still effectively engaged in pastoring and ministering in various ways.

And what about those who were simply caught up in the imminent rapture frenzy who lost faith and hope as the years passed, and who then grew old with no fulfillment of what they had been told was imminent? How many who came to Jesus during the Jesus Movement, and built their faith upon the faulty foundation of what they were led to believe was about to happen, now falter in faith and live in disappointment?

If we choose to cling to an unbiblical theology of defeated escapism, we will find ourselves passively waiting, gnawing on our own bitterness, disappointment, and depression, fearing the future and longing to escape, as opposed to walking in a winning spirit. We will have lost the battle before we even begin. In fact, we will be feeding another generational divide of the kind that happened during the Jesus Movement. Glory will be lost, just as it was back then. Fires will die.

God has ignited a movement of hope and victory in our day and it is taking root among young people. We older ones can let the young have it all by themselves and then watch it eventually die, or we can be the Joshuas and Calebs who lead the army of the young into a promised land and who feed on the strength God is sending.

## THE RAPTURE?

*For the Lord Himself will descend from heaven with a shout, with the voice of the archangel and with the trumpet of God, and the dead in Christ will rise first. Then we who are alive and remain will be caught up together with them in the clouds to meet the Lord in the air, and so we shall always be with the Lord* (1 Thessalonians 4:16-17).

Know for certain that I believe Scripture clearly teaches a coming rapture. We will be caught up to meet Him as He comes with those who've died before, and we will all be changed, "in a moment, in the twinkling of an eye, at the last trumpet; for the trumpet will sound, and the dead will be raised imperishable, and we will be changed" (1 Cor. 15:52). At that point, the earth will be redeemed and reborn, and we will rule with Jesus upon it.

First, however, we win, the nations are touched, multitudes come to Jesus, we shine like the sun, the wicked are gathered out and the righteous shine forth. I'm not saying that we will literally take over the world's governments, the seven mountains of influence, and establish the kingdom of God on earth by our own effort. I am no adherent of Dominionism. Whenever men have thought they could establish the kingdom of God on earth through earthly governments and man's efforts, it hasn't worked out well. You wouldn't want to have lived in Calvin's Geneva or in the Puritan colonies in America. In both cases, oppression and violation resulted. So-called Christian governments have always fallen first into the religious spirit and then descended into oppression and even cruelty.

I *am* saying that Jesus's kingdom is not of this earth, at least not the earth as we know it. Never was He interested in a worldly kingdom. I'm saying, nevertheless, that we have been called and equipped to infiltrate every arena of life and human endeavor to exert real influence, revealing who Jesus is and changing the atmosphere around us just by being who we are. This opens the hearts of people to receive Jesus through our ministry.

As I have said, prior to the return of the Lord and the rapture of the saints, we will see a great outpouring of God's Spirit and a tremendous harvest of souls coming to Jesus and being transformed. Love wins in a loveless age and a godless culture. Darkness never conquers light.

The idea that we will be raptured away, abandoning earth to destruction, is defeatist, but Jesus didn't call us to defeat. He called us to victory. Victory was paid for at the cross, established in the resurrection of Jesus and empowered on the Day of Pentecost when the Holy Spirit fell upon the gathered disciples.

Peter clearly spoke of the power bestowed on us for victory. "Peter said to them, 'Repent, and each of you be baptized in the name of Jesus Christ for the forgiveness of your sins; and you will receive the gift of the Holy Spirit. For the promise is for you and your children and for all who are far off, as many as the Lord our God will call to Himself'" (Acts 2:38-39). We get to win!

CHAPTER 3

# THE MILLENNIUM: REVELATION 20

THE IDEA OF THE MILLENNIAL REIGN OF CHRIST HAS always been confusing, controversial, and difficult. Whole denominations have split and gone their separate ways over differences of interpretation. My own problem in the study of the millennial reign of Jesus is that biblical eschatology, the study of the events of the last days, works well until you introduce a literal thousand-year reign into it. Simply stated, basic eschatology says that 1) Jesus comes. 2) Jesus dies. 3) Jesus is resurrected. 4) Jesus ascends into heaven. 5) Jesus comes again to judge the living and the dead after a period of tribulation, at which time we who remain alive are caught up to be with Him and are changed while those who have "fallen asleep" are raised, all of us imperishable. The wicked are resurrected, as well, but unto judgment. 6) Jesus casts Satan and his angels into the lake of fire along with the unrighteous who refused to believe. 7) Heaven and earth are destroyed and recreated, and we all live happily ever after with redeemed and perfected hearts on a redeemed earth. Inject a literal millennium into this summary and you have trouble making it fit. Things come unraveled.

## THREE VIEWS REVIEWED

### Premillennialism

Premillennialists see the millennium as a literal, rather than symbolic, period of time. Jesus returns to inaugurate the millennium, His thousand-year reign on earth, hence the "pre" element of the term. Most commonly associated with Dispensationalism, premillennialism sees history as divided into ages or dispensations in which God does particular things. For instance, this view holds that miracles ceased with the end of the apostolic age and the completion of the canon of Scripture. A "dispensation" ended.

According to premillennialists, God has two redemptive plans, one for literal Israel and another for Gentiles during the "church age." When the church age ends (usually associated with the seven churches of Revelation and the day of the Gentiles) and the church is raptured, the Jews who remain on earth will convert and receive Jesus.

This requires a pre-tribulation rapture with a secret return of the Lord, not visible to the entire world, followed by a visible return of the Lord after the Great Tribulation. The restoration of Israel as a nation becomes part of this prophetic scenario, together with the re-emergence of the Roman Empire in Europe and a Russian/Arab invasion of Israel—signs of the approach of the end times and the secret return of Jesus to rapture the church.

While I would say that the restoration of Israel was obviously a product of divine intervention and obviously a fulfillment of promises made by God, I don't think Scripture justifies seeing it as a reliable or predictable timeline for the return of Jesus. Nothing I've seen written along those lines has ever worked out.

The establishment of Israel also aroused the wrath of the entire Arab world, something not only embedded in biblical prophecies, but an extension of the millennia-old conflict between the sons of Ishmael and the sons of Isaac. Connecting the Israeli/Arab conflict with the return of Jesus, however, also seems questionable scripturally.

Europe, for its part, is no revived Roman Empire and Russia has no interest in invading Israel. They have nothing to gain by doing so. In short, no proposed or supposed sequence of events connecting the return of Jesus to the founding of the current state of Israel has ever panned out.

I will state, however, that God clearly deals with His people on the basis of their relationship to Him. He deals with nations on the basis of their relationship to His people. This includes both the church and literal Israel. While it may not relate directly to the return of Jesus, the future of the nations of the world turns heavily on how they choose to treat Israel and the church.

Premillennialists expect a rebuilt temple and reinstitution of the sacrificial system. In 1976, I took a seminary course on Judaism and Christianity. One of the most prominent conservative rabbis in the Los Angeles area came to speak. One question asked was, "We hear the Jews are planning to rebuild the temple. Is that true?" He answered firmly, "We don't need a temple. We don't need animal sacrifice. We have repentance." Many students of biblical history would say that the prophecies of the rebuilding of the temple were fulfilled one-to-one upon the return from the Babylonian exile and we need not look for a repeat.

In premillennialism, Jesus will rule the nations on earth during the thousand years, but the church (those who believed during the church age) will have been taken to heaven. But how does that fit with First Thessalonians 4:14-17?

*For if we believe that Jesus died and rose again, even so God will bring with Him those who have fallen asleep in Jesus. For this we say to you by the word of the Lord, that we who are alive and remain until the coming of the Lord, will not precede those*

*who have fallen asleep. For the Lord Himself will
descend from heaven with a shout, with the voice of
the archangel and with the trumpet of God, and the
dead in Christ will rise first. Then we who are alive
and remain will be caught up together with them
in the clouds to meet the Lord in the air, and so we
shall always be with the Lord.*

Inject a literal, Dispensational, premillennial interpretation
into this and it all falls apart. It just doesn't fit the framework
of the rest of the Bible. Better, therefore, to look for a more
symbolic meaning in keeping with the nature of apocalyptic
literature. Please review Chapter One for a basic explanation
of premillennialism, postmillennialism, and amillennialism. I
will not give a broad examination of postmillennialism here,
except to say it fits well with Dominionism, the idea that we
will establish the kingdom of God on earth by Spirit-inspired
human effort and then deliver it up to Jesus at His coming.
Hence, according to postmillennialism, Jesus will return
after the thousand-year reign to receive His kingdom. I will,
however, suggest a simple solution to the millennial problem,
best categorized as an amillennial view that brings the victory
we have in Jesus into the present.

### Amillennialism

*Amillennialism* essentially means "no literal millennium."
For most of church history until the rise of Dispensationalism
in the early nineteenth century, the amillennial view has been
the dominant position of the church. What follows is my version, not too different from the historical mainstream prior to
about 1830. My view turns on the biblical assertion, seen in the

words of Jesus and the other New Testament books, that the kingdom of God is present in the here and now. This assertion is either true, or Jesus lied, which is not a possibility any of us would entertain.

Foundational to the message of the gospel as Jesus and the apostles preached it is the fact that the kingdom of God is at hand. Matthew 12:28 quotes Jesus as saying, "But if I cast out demons by the Spirit of God, then the kingdom of God has come upon you." Even more significant is Mark 9:1, "Truly I say to you, there are some of those who are standing here who will not taste death until they see the kingdom of God after it has come with power." In the book of Acts, Jesus told the disciples, "but you will receive power when the Holy Spirit has come upon you; and you shall be My witnesses both in Jerusalem, and in all Judea and Samaria, and even to the remotest part of the earth" (Acts 1:8). In fulfillment of those words, the Holy Spirit fell on the 120 in the Upper Room just ten days after Jesus ascended to heaven. Later, in the power of that original outpouring, Paul "entered the synagogue and continued speaking out boldly for three months, reasoning and persuading them about the kingdom of God" (Acts 19:8).

In every case, the words of both Jesus and the apostles affirmed the truth that the rule and reign of Jesus has come to earth and is present with us now. We live in the already/not yet when the present age and the age to come overlap while we await the fullness at Jesus's coming when the present age will end and only the kingdom of God will remain. Meanwhile, we get to live in the kingdom to minister and enjoy the powers of the age to come, winning people, changing cultures, and influencing nations. Holy Spirit moves among us, love multiplies where His nature is truly understood and received, and signs, wonders, and healings flow from the heart of the Father. Doesn't that sound like victory?

Clearly Jesus announced that the kingdom of God would come with power within the lifetimes of those listening to Him (see Mark 9:1). The only possible candidate for the fulfillment of that prophetic word is the day of Pentecost when the power of the Holy Spirit fell on them in the Upper Room (see Acts 2). The number 1,000 in the thousand-year reign is best taken as symbolic of an extended period of time set by God in which we, as believers, walk in kingdom power and love. Our mandate and purpose is to influence and disciple nations. We are light and life in a dark world that ceases to be dark wherever our presence is felt and seen.

Notwithstanding the fact that mankind has never been able to live out the principles of the kingdom of God governmentally, it remains true that from the time of Jesus until now Christian influence has shaped the stated values and practices of the governments of the world. Apocalyptic language expresses things in extremes and absolutes consistent with the dream/vision state from which they flow. So, in a very real sense, since the time of Jesus's ministry, and especially the day of Pentecost, the kingdom of God has been present on earth and, more than any other factor, has influenced all the nations of the earth, regardless of how badly those nations may have twisted it up or misapplied it. And this doesn't even begin to address the presence of the Holy Spirit in demonstrations of power through believers in every age from Bible times until now.

Further, the majority of the world has been favorable toward Christianity as a faith from A.D. 314 until now. In our day, however, this is changing. As we approach the return of the Lord, Satan is being released from his bonds. From the time of Jesus until now, theologians have said that Satan has been bound, but with a long rope. In the last days, the days of the Great Tribulation, restrictions are lifted and he is free to throw one last temper tantrum against the Lord's people, knowing that he has but a short time before his ultimate and final demise. Still, we prevail in victory in the midst.

In the sense that I'm describing, we have been living in the millennium from the time of Jesus, at least since the Day of Pentecost, until now. It is the already/not yet. Only by looking at it in this way does all the eschatology seem to fit.

You might be wondering how this fits the victory theme of this book, if you haven't already seen it. If the kingdom of God is truly present, then in some sense the rule and reign of God are here now. In Jesus we have the privilege of ministering that power, demonstrating the Lordship of Jesus, to a world in need. Not only do we have the power of testimony in the midst of all forms of darkness and against all opposition, we have the anointing of God to demonstrate the kingdom in miracles of mercy and love. The sick are healed, the lame walk, and the blind see. In and through touches of the kingdom of God, people come to Jesus and lives are changed. Victory! A great harvest of souls before the return of Jesus! And the faithful ultimately inherit the earth to rule and reign with Him!

Additionally, shouldn't we be using our gifts to benefit governments, employers, and others in authority? Shouldn't believers in Jesus be recognized as the most valuable people in society to have on anyone's team? Like Joseph in Egypt, who interpreted Pharaoh's dream and proposed a wise plan to prepare and survive a coming famine, shouldn't we be sought out by employers and government officials for our gifts and our wisdom? Pharaoh promoted Joseph from prison to a positon of authority second only to his own. Shouldn't we be similarly placed, and for similar reasons? Rather than waiting and hoping for escape, shouldn't we be ruling and reigning?

In February 2018, Billy Graham passed away. By virtue of love, anointing, and integrity, he ministered to a succession of presidents of the United States from both sides of the political spectrum in addition to winning untold numbers of people to salvation in our Lord. We have come into a period of history in which a new crop of Holy Spirit-filled Christians must arise to influence governments, business leaders, and civic organizations. My own wife, on a more local and simple level, has befriended cashiers in grocery stores and won the right to pray for them. In one case, this resulted in a Walmart worker's mother receiving a healing for life-threatening diabetes. In another instance, my wife presented herself as a servant in a grade school to help teachers in setting up classrooms. Having thus won the respect and trust of the school principal and staff, she was not only allowed to pray through the halls of the school but was given lists of specific student needs to take to our children at church for prayer. Change resulted. This is victory and this is influence, the reign of Jesus on earth.

## SYMBOLISM UNPACKED

*Then I saw an angel coming down from heaven, holding the key of the abyss and a great chain in his hand. And he laid hold of the dragon, the serpent of old, who is the devil and Satan, and bound him for a thousand years (Revelation 20:1-2).*

### A Thousand Years

As a symbolic number, 1,000 stands for a long period of time. Alternatively, we can break it down as a multiple of three tens: 10x10x10 = 1,000. The number 3 points to the Trinity, our triune God, fully one and yet fully three. Ten is a number of fullness. We are therefore looking at a God-ordained fullness of time, rather than a literal number of years.

### Satan Has Been Bound

> [The angel] threw him into the abyss, and shut it and sealed it over him, so that he would not deceive the nations any longer, until the thousand years were completed; after these things he must be released for a short time (Revelation 20:3).

Satan is bound, but how? Since Jesus broke the power of the devil and his angels by the cross and resurrection, Satan has been bound, but with a long chain as the theologians sometimes say. Jesus secured his defeat at the cross and by the victory of the resurrection.

> When you were dead in your transgressions and the uncircumcision of your flesh, He made you alive together with Him, having forgiven us all our transgressions, having canceled out the certificate of debt consisting of decrees against us, which was hostile to us; and He has taken it out of the way, having nailed it to the cross. When He had disarmed the rulers and authorities, He made a public display

*of them, having triumphed over them through Him*
(Colossians 2:13-15).

The idea that Satan can no longer deceive the nations means at least that he is powerless to prevent Christian influence from spreading into every nation on earth, as it has certainly done and is doing. The values of nearly every government on earth, even when twisted and distorted into an evil form, have been shaped by the gospel.

### Released for a Short Time

Just at the end, Satan is released for a short time. I believe this is the basis for the Great Tribulation. Satan rages, knowing that he has only a short time to do as much damage as possible. This, however, is only so that he can at last be thoroughly and finally broken. We must learn to regard Satan as the defeated foe that he truly is and stop fearing him as some kind of powerful adversary.

This fits Second Thessalonians 2:7-8: "For the mystery of lawlessness is already at work; only he who now restrains will do so until he is taken out of the way. Then that lawless one will be revealed whom the Lord will slay with the breath of His mouth and bring to an end by the appearance of His coming." Here we see the restraint placed on Satan and his minions, as well as the idea that at some point they will be released, exposed, and defeated. At every point, Scripture presents us with victory.

It would be important to note that the context of the passage does not indicate that the church will have been evacuated when all this comes to pass. Because both the church of Thessalonica and the apostle clearly believed the end times were upon them, Paul was speaking to that Gentile church about what would happen to them. He was informing them what to look for in their present lives, not what would happen after they were gone. The fact that Jesus did not return within their lifetimes in no way diminishes the truth of what the apostle had to say about end-time events. He might have been wrong in his underlying assumptions, which he never clearly stated as a teaching, but his words ring true for what must eventually transpire.

### Resurrections

> Then I saw thrones, and they sat on them, and judgment was given to them. And I saw the souls of those who had been beheaded because of their testimony of Jesus and because of the word of God, and those who had not worshiped the beast or his image, and had not received the mark on their forehead and on their hand; and they came to life and reigned with Christ for a thousand years. The rest of the dead did not come to life until the thousand years were completed. This is the first resurrection (Revelation 20:4-5).

Historically, beheading has not been a common punishment for heresy or for refusal to buy into an opposing religion. Is it not interesting that radical Islamists now use it as a common means of execution for those they consider infidels? At the very least, the statement that they "came to life and reigned with Christ for a thousand years" points once more to the ultimate victory and to the certainty of our own resurrection regardless of the possibility of earthly martyrdom. Consider, as well, Ephesians 2:6 where the apostle says that we have been seated with Christ—stated as present reality—in the heavenly places where Jesus sits at the right hand of God.

No other place in Scripture mentions two resurrections, save perhaps First Thessalonians 4:16 with reference to the second coming, "For the Lord Himself will descend from heaven with a shout, with the voice of the archangel and with the trumpet of God, and the dead in Christ will rise first." Even then, however, the context indicates that "first" means only that this resurrection is just the first of two connected events. "Then we who are alive and remain will be caught up together with them in the clouds to meet the Lord in the air, and so we shall always be with the Lord" (1 Thess. 4:17).

A clearer reference would be John 3:36: "He who believes in the Son has eternal life." The word *has* is present tense. In effect, we have been raised from the dead to eternal life the moment we believe. New life has come. We are born again. In that light, the second resurrection would be the resurrection of the physical body unto the judgment at the end of the age, the end of the millennium—the moment of reward for believers and punishment of the wicked.

See also First Corinthians 15:22-24:

> *For as in Adam all die, so also in Christ all will be made alive. But each in his own order: Christ the first fruits, after that those who are Christ's at His coming, then comes the end, when He hands over the kingdom to the God and Father, when He has abolished all rule and all authority and power.*

Life has been granted to us now and in eternity, as well as authority and power for victory on this earth. Our lives affect those around us. The gospel goes forth victoriously even in the midst of trial. Our hope transcends all circumstances. Historically, the Christians won the Roman Empire. "For we are a fragrance of Christ to God among those who are being saved and among those who are perishing; to the one an aroma from death to death, to the other an aroma from life to life. And who is adequate for these things?" (2 Cor. 2:15-16). The biblical promise and mandate is for victory, not escape.

"Blessed and holy is the one who has a part in the first resurrection; over these the second death has no power, but they will be priests of God and of Christ and will reign with Him for a thousand years" (Rev. 20:6). Clearly, the first resurrection occurs when we are born again, resurrected from death to life. This gives us power over the second death. The first death is the death of the body. The second death is hell and alienation from the presence of God.

"When the thousand years are completed, Satan will be released from his prison" (Rev. 20:7). This points back to Second Thessalonians 2:7-8: "He who now restrains will do so until he is taken out of the way." It would seem that different writers, receiving the same word under different anointings and in different situations, expressed the same truths in varying terms.

Revelation 20:8-9 speaks of Gog and Magog gathering the forces of the nations to come against the saints in the beloved city, stating simply that fire came and devoured them. Again, apocalyptic literature speaks in symbolic terms, often explainable by other passages of Scripture. Here we see rising universal opposition to Christianity. "The number of them is like the sand of the seashore" indicates widespread opposition. "The beloved city" represents believers. "Fire devoured them" says that God will consume the opposition. In prophetic perspective, this represents the events that led to the eventual victory of Christianity under the Roman Empire as well as to a greater thing yet to come that is foreshadowed and completed in the depth of the prophecy.

John prophesied a widespread revulsion toward Christianity in the end times following a period of acceptance. This has been true in modern times. In America alone, we have seen a transition from defining the nation as "Christian" to a growing rejection of that premise, even to the point of many on the left seeing Christianity as a threat. John foresaw ultimate victory and redemption for believers on this earth, regardless of opposition. This was the hope of the early Christians and this is the hope of believers in our time. We get to win.

Revelation 20:10-11 paints a picture of the devil and all his minions being cast into eternal destruction and torment while Jesus assumes the throne. Verses 12 and those that follow show us the final judgment of men and women.

What we see at the end of it all is destruction of the entire corrupted created order, soon to be replaced with a new one (see 2 Pet. 3:13). On this renewed and redeemed earth, we rule and reign with Jesus, having walked victoriously in this world until His return.

## SUMMARY

Revelation 20 is a partial rewind that reviews the end-time events once more from yet another perspective with a focus on the finality. In Jesus's earthly ministry Satan was cast down and bound. "But if I cast out demons by the Spirit of God, then the kingdom of God has come upon you. Or how can anyone enter the strong man's house and carry off his property, unless he first binds the strong man? And then he will plunder his house" (Matt. 12:28-29). This is the beginning of the millennial rule. In Jesus we plunder what the devil thought was his.

As Satan is bound/limited for these many years—the symbolic 1,000—Christian influence fills the earth, represented as the "rule" of Christ. Every government system on earth has been influenced directly or indirectly by Christian values, while every government ever raised up against Christ and Christian values has ultimately fallen, either to dominance by Christianity or to destruction.

Our salvation in Jesus constitutes the first resurrection as we who believe have been transferred from death to life. In the second resurrection, we move into eternal life, or in the case of the unrighteous unbelieving, the judgment of hell and eternal alienation from God in the lake of fire.

Corresponding to the period of the Great Tribulation, Satan will be released, unbound, in order to oppose believers with a rising opposition to the gospel and those who stand for it—culminating in what might be called Armageddon—but only so that he may at last be destroyed when the Lord returns and we join Him in victory.

The thousand years of the millennial reign began with Jesus's ministry on earth and took real root on the day of Pentecost when those who were alive during Jesus's lifetime saw the kingdom come with power. Since that time, the will of heaven has been done on earth in signs and wonders and in Christian influence spreading through the nations. We have been living in the millennial reign of Christ and should be walking in its power and authority today. We win!

CHAPTER 4

# THINGS WE'VE BEEN TAUGHT TO FEAR

# THE MARK OF THE BEAST

Isn't it time to stop all the hysteria over the mark of the beast? Those who allow themselves to be caught up in the fear of microchips implanted in their hands or foreheads have missed the point, not having been educated concerning the historical and cultural forces at work at the time that John wrote Revelation or the Jewish practices and symbols involved. I mean no condemnation or judgment. We can't blame most people who don't have time to research things deeply for believing what they see in print. There's simply been too much fear-mongering published by those who really don't know or understand. Unfortunately, it does generate excitement and attract a lot of attention.

The apostle John wrote:

> *And he causes all, the small and the great, and the rich and the poor, and the free men and the slaves, to be given a mark on their right hand or on their forehead, and he provides that no one will be able to buy or to sell, except the one who has the mark, either the name of the beast or the number of his name* (Revelation 13:16-17).

What was he actually saying to first- and second-century Christians, and what might it have to do with the time in which we live? Deuteronomy 6:6-8 reads:

> *These words, which I am commanding you today, shall be on your heart. You shall teach them diligently to your sons and shall talk of them when*

*you sit in your house and when you walk by the way
and when you lie down and when you rise up. You
shall bind them as a sign on your hand and they
shall be as frontals on your forehead.*

In Bible times, in literal obedience to this instruction, every Jewish man would begin the day by binding a small leather box on his hand and another on his forehead. These would contain a few lines of Scripture. Even today, orthodox Jews carry this daily ritual forward to mark themselves as covenanted to God and walking in subjection to His Word.

To illustrate the point, I once found myself waiting to board an early morning flight to London just at sunrise. A Jewish man in orthodox garb and the long ear locks, worn by eastern European orthodox Jews, stood facing the rising sun as it shone through the floor-to-ceiling window in the waiting area by the gate. Rocking back and forth in prayer, he donned his phylacteries—one leather box on his hand, secured by straps up his forearm, and the other on his forehead.

Understand that, as apocalyptic literature, Revelation is a book written in code, filled with symbols and metaphors familiar to its intended audience and never meant to be taken literally. Every first- and second-century Jewish person reading this passage would have understood references to the mark on the forehead and the hand and called up the mental image of a man wearing his phylacteries to declare his devotion to God.

John wrote symbolically concerning a specific situation faced by believers who lived in his day. Consider, therefore, that in many cities of the Roman Empire, one had to belong to a trade guild in order to do business. Each guild worshiped a patron god from the pantheon of Roman deities. Meetings were held in the temples of those deities where they offered sacrifices to the patron gods of those guilds. The meetings included feasts, often followed by orgies. Obviously, no Christian could participate in such things and could not therefore legally ply a trade. In other words, they could not buy or sell.

In that light, the mark of the beast points not to a literal mark but rather to a system in which standing for one's faith, being marked by God as belonging to Him in covenant, could exact an economic penalty. Obviously, considering the history from which the symbolism is drawn, a microchip embedded in someone's hand is a stretch too far. The language speaks symbolically to what happened in John's day and perhaps yet to come in our own time when failure to declare loyalty or obedience to an ungodly system might mean loss of income or even business closure. Already, in my own city of Denver, Colorado, a cake shop owner has been successfully sued by a gay couple for refusing, for the sake of Christian conscience, to make a wedding cake for their same-sex marriage celebration. Similar suits have been filed and won in other U.S. cities as well. We have seen county clerks and justices of the peace under persecution for refusing to grant marriage licenses to gay couples. Praise God that the U.S. Supreme Court recently upheld the right of that cake shop owner to refuse service, but the process of appeal was long and arduous.

How many of us have paid a price for bringing a Bible to the workplace? Or for speaking out about Jesus in the public school system? Forget about microchips. The more likely scenario is the one I'm describing, symbolically represented by "the mark" and applicable to our own day as well as to John's.

This is prophetic perspective—one historical fulfillment followed by a greater one in the fullness of the original word.

Think of it another way. Why would any person or government go to the expense, and weather the public outcry, to insert a chip in anyone's hand, much less on the forehead, when the world is turning to much more efficient and reliable fingerprint technology, facial recognition software, and even iris recognition?

# THE ANTICHRIST

If you have been fearing the rise of the antichrist, please stop. I will say simply that it's probably not what you think it is or who you might suppose it to be. Even more, why attribute more power to an antichrist figure than we do to Jesus our Lord? Or do we truly believe that Jesus is, in fact, Lord? Fear points to the presence of some degree of unbelief in the power and sovereignty of the God we serve.

See Revelation 13:18: "Here is wisdom. Let him who has understanding calculate the number of the beast, for the number is that of a man; and his number is six hundred and sixty-six." The ancient world didn't use the Arabic numerals we employ today. Instead, they used letters of the alphabet to indicate numerical values in a system called *gematria*. Even today we use Roman numerals, letters of the Latin alphabet, only to date movie releases and Super Bowls, but for literally nothing else. In the ancient world, anyone's name could therefore be represented numerically by adding up the values of the letters in the name. Ancient graffiti, for instance, have been found carved into stone with statements like, "John loves she whose number is 585."

No one has ever been able to identify any literal person in history whose name could be numerically represented by 666. The problem with attempting to apply 666 to anyone in John's day is that it corresponds to no known historical leader or emperor. The name "Nero," the evil emperor who used Christians dipped in tar as torches at his garden parties, almost fits, but only if misspelled in Latin as "Neron."

The issue gets worse when you try to apply the number of a name to anyone in modern times. We no longer use *gematria* to calculate numerical values. Further, in the original Greek, there is no definite article in front of *man*. It can therefore be translated either as "a man" or simply as "man," but not "the man." In other words, 666 can be understood as the number of "man" in general. If it is the number of man in general, then it would indicate a time when man deifies himself and rejects God—a time when mankind makes its own rules and exalts the human spirit, or a time when the majority become conditioned to believe that we're all good people and therefore will go to heaven. And what about all those who want to believe that we are all little christs, extensions of deity? If 666 refers to a specific man, then we have a problem because it becomes nearly impossible to identify who that man might be, either from John's day or in our own.

Perhaps more telling is John's own definition of "the" anti-christ. "Who is the liar but the one who denies that Jesus is the Christ? This is the antichrist, the one who denies the Father and the Son" (1 John 2:22). John penned the Revelation as well as First John. He identifies the antichrist specifically as the spirit that denies the incarnation of Jesus, God become man. He said it again in First John 4:2-3, "By this you know the Spirit of God: every spirit that confesses that Jesus Christ has come in the flesh is from God; and every spirit that does not con-fess Jesus is not from God; this is the spirit of the antichrist, of which you have heard that it is coming, and now it is already in the world." In Second John 1:7 he made the same point: "For many deceivers have gone out into the world, those who do not acknowledge Jesus Christ as coming in the flesh. This is the deceiver and the antichrist." One of the key debates in the early church had to do with the incarnation. Did God truly become flesh? Or did He only seem or appear to do so? Or was it simply that God took an ordinary man and adopted him? The former is what we call Docetism, while the latter is Adoptionism. John saw both of these heresies developing and warned against them, calling them "antichrist."

In other words, we could safely identify "the" antichrist as Satan, who seeks to undermine the truth that God became flesh in Jesus in order to save us. The battle over that foundational element of our faith formed the core of many of the early church's doctrinal debates. Greek philosophy had invaded the Roman world. In Greek thought, flesh was seen as evil. The idea that God would defile Himself by having anything to do with it seemed inconceivable.

The antichrist now works in Islam, Judaism, Buddhism and other faiths in which the idea of God becoming man is seen as anathema. The secular world merely sneers at the idea with no religious reason for doing so.

My point? Settle down and stop feeding fear. No attempt to identify the antichrist as a specific man has ever resulted in a workable conclusion. In short, "antichrist" is first a spirit—Satan himself, in my opinion—that denies the true identity and nature of Jesus, His divinity, and the reality of His incarnation.

Nevertheless, attempts to identify who this antichrist might be continue to proliferate. As I grew up in the midst of the frenzy over the soon return of Jesus and impending rapture that infused the Jesus Movement, I saw numerous efforts to identify some living person as the antichrist. For example, as noted earlier in this book, in the early 1970s both the prince of Spain and Henry Kissinger were put forward as candidates who supposedly fit all the signs. More recently, people have tried to lay it on Barack Obama or even the current Pope. It just doesn't work!

In the coming days, we must choose to walk in our appointed glory as we focus not on the antichrist, the mark of the beast, or any other distraction, but rather on the face of Jesus. "But we all, with unveiled face, beholding as in a mirror the glory of the Lord, are being transformed into the same image from glory to glory, just as from the Lord, the Spirit" (2 Cor. 3:18).

## THE TWO BEASTS AND THE ONE WORLD GOVERNMENT

Revelation 13 speaks of two beasts, one coming up from the sea with ten horns and seven heads on which were blasphemous names, and the other having two horns like a lamb and speaking as a dragon. Some—mostly those who see Revelation as entirely a book of future prophecies yet to be fulfilled—believe this to be the coming emergence of a one-world government with the antichrist at its head.

Remember, however, that historical context informs meaning. By the time John wrote the Revelation, emperor worship had taken root in the Roman Empire. This arose as a popular response of gratitude for the *Pax Romana*, the

Peace of Rome. Prior to Rome establishing its rule over the whole of the Mediterranean Basin, brigands, thieves, and pirates made trade difficult, if not impossible. Travel and the transportation of goods were dangerous pursuits. As a result, everyone suffered economically and in other ways. The rise of Rome to dominance brought peace and stability as the empire constructed roads for commerce and Roman power enforced safety on the sea and land. The empire prospered, and with it all the nations and people groups it encompassed.

Not only did Rome worship a pantheon of gods, but, as prosperity grew, people began to exalt the "genius" or the spirit of Rome, personified and embodied in the emperor. Some emperors actually began to respond to this by openly claiming divinity. In some cities and regions of the empire, the law required every subject of the realm to sacrifice a pinch of incense annually to the emperor and declare, "Caesar is Lord." Christians, of course, could not do so—Jesus alone is Lord— and were therefore branded as subversives, disloyal to the Roman state. At the cost of their livelihoods and sometimes their lives, they stood their ground.

Beast number one, therefore, symbolically represents the Roman Empire and its government arising from the masses of people symbolized by the sea. Beast number two represents the pagan religious system with its worship of the emperor. As the second beast rode upon the back of the first beast, we understand that the pagan system of worship, imposed upon Christians and practiced in the empire, was supported and enforced by the government of Rome—a religious beast bound together with and empowered by a governmental beast.

Is this picture of a one world government with its religious system limited to John's day under the Romans? Or might there be an element of prophetic perspective involved in which there may yet be a greater fulfillment reflective of the first one that manifested in John's day? The answer remains unclear.

Why do I question this? In contrast to the Roman Empire of John's day, current trends point not to the growth of a one world government, but to increasing division and fragmentation, and I find nothing in Scripture that would compel me to conclude that a one world government applies to anything but the historical situation in John's day. The United Nations is an impotent organization functioning as little more than a platform for the nations of the world to argue and hurl accusations at one another—and especially at Israel. It seems that every ethnic group seeks to become its own nation. The Soviet Union is no more, its various member nations now functioning as independent states. The European Union includes many more than ten nations, and even some of those nations appear to be increasingly restive under its dominion. Witness the exit of the United Kingdom! A one world government hardly seems likely in light of the trend to fragmentation around the world. This alone should allay our misguided fears and put to rest a raft of conspiracy theories.

Could it be that our modern version of the two beasts can be found in the growing influence of political correctness and the legal penalties visited upon those who will not bow the knee to its godless principles? Could it be that the penalties visited upon Christian businesses that refuse to compromise biblical mandates and values represent a measure of what John foresaw, especially if prophetic perspective is involved? Could it be that a modern version of the Roman system could be reflected in job losses suffered by believers who refuse agreement with certain ungodly leftist philosophies? Could it be that the image of the second beast appearing as a lamb and the image of the resurrected beast in Revelation 13:14 reflect the truncated and compromised version of Christianity growing in our culture that claims to worship Jesus, but clearly not the real Jesus of the biblical record?

In any case, we must not allow these things to consume our attention. We must rather seek a purity of focus on who Jesus truly is, gazing into His face, being transformed by His glory. Do this, and we will win, no matter what happens in the world around us or what pressures may come against us. What is clear is that deep darkness will cover the peoples, but the glory of the Lord will rise upon us. Once more, no matter the world condition, we arise victorious.

# CHAPTER 5

# THE PRE-TRIB ORIGIN AND OTHER MISCONCEPTIONS

I N THE EARLY 1800s, A CHARISMATIC REVIVAL BROKE OUT in Scotland and England. It included prophecy, dreams, visions, and the gift of tongues. In the midst of this, in Port Glasgow, Scotland, a young woman, Margaret McDonald, suffering from a grave illness received and experienced a revelatory vision.

Eyewitness Rev. Robert Norton reported the content of what she saw. First, she said that her vision prophesied the coming of the Lord. Second, she stated that the sign of the Son of Man is not to be seen by the human eye but is rather the filling of believers with the Holy Spirit as the Lord descends from heaven with a shout. She referred to First Thessalonians 4:13-14,16-17:

> *But we do not want you to be uninformed, brethren, about those who are asleep, so that you will not grieve as do the rest who have no hope. For if we believe that Jesus died and rose again, even so God will bring with Him those who have fallen asleep in Jesus. ...For the Lord Himself will descend from heaven with a shout, with the voice of the archangel and with the trumpet of God, and the dead in Christ will rise first. Then we who are alive and remain will be caught up together with them in the clouds to meet the Lord in the air, and so we shall always be with the Lord.*

According to Reverend Norton, she believed that only those who have the light of God within them would be able to see that sign because it is spiritually discerned. This is likely where the idea of a secret return of the Lord to rapture the saints prior to the Great Tribulation was born, although this doesn't appear to be what she meant. Obviously, there were problems with her statement, not the least of which would be Revelation 1:7: "Behold, He is coming with the clouds, and every eye will see Him, even those who pierced Him; and all the tribes of the earth will mourn over Him."

Well-meaning folks who experience genuine encounters with God do often spiritualize passages of Scripture or turn them into metaphors for things other than the intended meaning of the text when trying to make sense of what they have experienced. Predictably, this produces flawed results, as it did with Margaret McDonald. So her experience was real, but the interpretation of her experience was off. Especially in times of revival, we must learn to interpret experience in light of the Scriptures rather than interpret the Scriptures in light of experience.

On the basis of her vision, Margaret McDonald believed that the spiritual temple, not a physical one, must be raised, built up, and then we would be caught up to meet Jesus. She tied this to Ephesians 5:27, "that He might present to Himself the church in all her glory, having no spot or wrinkle or any such thing; but that she would be holy and blameless" as well as First Peter 2:1-10 and Joel 2:28-31.

According to her vision, those filled with the Spirit are able to see and feel spiritual things, while others, because they are not in the Spirit, cannot. In this sense, she believed, two shall be in one bed, one taken and the other left, which reflects the aforementioned tendency to misinterpretation by means of spiritualizing and making a metaphor of Matthew 24:38-44, again divorced from the historical setting of the text and what it actually states. In Margaret McDonald's mind, all of this tied into First Corinthians 2:14, "But a natural man does not accept the things of the Spirit of God, for they are foolishness to him; and he cannot understand them, because they are spiritually appraised."

She believed that the people of God would be in a very dangerous situation when the Lord appears in this way. The wicked would wield the power to deceive so that a fiery ordeal would descend upon God's people. Persecution, she believed, would increase in direct proportion to the increase of the Holy Spirit and that this would shake every soul to its core. Passages she cited for support would be Matthew 24:9-11 and First Peter 4:12-19. Drawing from Matthew 24, she believed a false christ would soon appear in her day.

## COMMENTS ON MARGARET McDONALD'S VISION

In my opinion, Margaret McDonald foresaw in some sense the latter day outpouring of the Holy Spirit before the Great Tribulation that would prepare the body of Christ to successfully and victoriously navigate it. She believed that the Great Tribulation would purify the church. Times of persecution and pressure do tend to separate the lukewarm from the passionate. On both points, she had it right in some ways, but in too many cases she misapplied the Scriptures, spiritualizing many passages and treating others as metaphors, as opposed to binding herself to the actual meaning of the words in context. In so doing, she inadvertently loosed the idea of a secret coming of the Lord before the tribulation, not seen by those without spiritual discernment, at which time the saints would be raptured away, although this kind of rapture was not her own belief. Other people, inspired by a misunderstanding of her words, crafted and then released the pre-tribulation rapture teaching.

When the wrong scriptures are employed to teach even right doctrines, doors open for heretical teachings to emerge as those who latch on to those misapplications develop mutations of the original teachings. In every age, when the Lord revives His church through His Holy Spirit, He sends messengers to proclaim His coming in the outpouring of His Spirit. Margaret McDonald foresaw this, but unfortunately and unintentionally spawned a false teaching that she never would have espoused personally.

As an example of this kind of divine announcement of an impending move of the Spirit, at the tender of age of eight my own son knelt before the altar in tears during a worship service as a voice spoke to him, "I'm coming soon." Because we had not yet taught him concerning the return of Jesus, it was pure revelation. Hearing that kind of thing, in our fervent longing for the Lord's return, people often tend to assume that God must be speaking of the *parousia*, the return of Jesus and the revelation of who He is in glory. This can feed the hope that He will take us off this earth before real trouble develops. In most cases, however, encounters of this kind mean only that a fresh move of God is imminent. The word my son received announced such a coming move of God.

Assumptions of a pretribulation rapture to deliver us from a season of trial and trouble hold an obvious appeal. We therefore hear what we want to hear and insert into the text of Scripture what we want to see. If we're not grounded in the whole testimony of the Word of God, we'll twist it all up.

# Two Men Who Built on Margaret McDonald's Words

Two men took their cues from Margaret McDonald's misapplication of the Word to develop and promulgate unbiblical doctrines that Margaret McDonald never intended. No record exists of the church teaching a pretribulation rapture before the early 1800s. One might ask, if the Scriptures so clearly teach this, then why was it unheard of prior to about 1830? Some claim that the early church fathers taught a pretribulation rapture, but having read the passages cited from their writings, I think that one could only come to that conclusion by reading those writings through a preconceived filter.

### John Darby

John Darby fathered the doctrinal system we call Dispensationalism. Dispensationalism holds that certain actions of God are limited to their respective periods of history or "dispensations." When a dispensation ends, so do the actions or gifts of God designated for that period of time. For instance, dispensationalists teach that when the apostolic age ended and the canon of Scripture was complete, the gifts of the Spirit ceased. Their "dispensation" had ended. Thus, when the "church age" ends, the church will be raptured away and the Great Tribulation will begin.

Dispensationalism enabled Darby to propose, falsely, the existence of two separate peoples of God—the church and Israel—with separate redemptive histories and destinies. Gentiles would be converted prior to the rapture, while Jews would become believers in Jesus during the tribulation period after the removal of the church from the earth. This division of the church and Israel founders on the rocks of Paul's teaching in Romans 11 that both Jews and Gentiles are one in the same trunk of the spiritual olive tree. Jews are the natural branches while Gentiles have been grafted in. It's one tree, not two. It's one plan of salvation applicable to all, "to the Jew first and also to the Greek" (Rom. 1:16).

I find it curious that so many Christians who accept, believe in, and practice the miraculous gifts of the Spirit so easily adopt a doctrine of the rapture birthed in, and dependent on, Dispensational theology that denies the reality of those gifts today.

### Edward Irving

In his acceptance of tongues and prophecy, Edward Irving has generally been regarded as a forerunner of the Charismatic Renewal. He admitted that the doctrine of a pretribulation rapture cannot be found in Scripture and that it originated with a prophetess (Margaret McDonald) in the 1830s. Like Darby, he taught a secret coming to rapture the church before the unfolding of the seven years of tribulation. One can only assume that he had erroneously accepted an element of extra-biblical revelation as a solid truth because it appealed to him or seemed like revelation.

Both Darby and Irving knew Margaret McDonald. Both of them either misinterpreted her, misunderstood her, or took what they wanted from her visions and words in order to construct distinctive doctrines for personal gain and advancement. Neither of them accurately interpreted or applied the Scriptures with respect to the second coming of our Lord.

# THE TRUTH

In addition to the passages cited in Chapter 1, the following apply.

*Matthew 24:26-27*

Matthew 24:26-27 so clearly states, "So if they say to you, 'Behold, He is in the wilderness,' do not go out, or, 'Behold, He is in the inner rooms,' do not believe them. For just as the lightning comes from the east and flashes even to the west, so will the coming of the Son of Man be." In other words, no hint of a secret coming to rapture the saints away prior to the Great Tribulation can be found in anything Jesus said. In Matthew 24 He warned the disciples not to accept claims of any kind that Jesus had returned if those claims of return did not conform to the parameters of His own words. Unless they saw Him appearing openly like lightning in the sky that all could witness, they were to reject any claims that He had come at all. There could, therefore, be no secret coming. Pretribulation rapture theory requires that we believe in two returns—one to take the saints off the earth and the other at the end of the tribulation period in final judgment—but the words of Jesus quite clearly rule this out.

*Revelation 7:13-14*

In His vision of the end times, the apostle John saw and wrote the same truth previously embedded in the words of Jesus in Matthew 24, that believers will not escape the Great Tribulation but rather live victoriously through it.

*Then one of the elders answered, saying to me, "These who are clothed in the white robes, who are they, and where have they come from?" I said to him, "My lord, you know." And he said to me, "These are the ones who come out of the great tribulation, and they have washed their robes and made them white in the blood of the Lamb"* (Revelation 7:13-14).

How could they come "out of" the Great Tribulation if they had not been "in" it? Pre-tribbers would assert that these are the Jewish believers converted after the church is raptured, but this requires that secret coming of the Lord that Jesus so clearly rules out. A further problem lies with the usual accompanying teaching that the Holy Spirit—as the restraining one—is taken off the earth as well during this post-rapture period. But First Corinthians 12:3 so clearly states that no one can say Jesus is Lord without the Holy Spirit. It would therefore be impossible for anyone to come to Jesus and recognize Him as Lord in a time when the Holy Spirit had vacated the earth. The entire pre-trib rapture argument comes unraveled on multiple fronts when examined in light of the whole of Scripture.

# THE SEVEN CHURCHES OF REVELATION

In Revelation 2 and 3, John wrote to seven real churches in "Asia," now known to us as Turkey. The text reflects very real situations those churches faced in the first century. In the letters to those churches, John drew his metaphors from actual conditions, obstacles, and pagan influences that existed in those cities at that time.

Some pretribulation rapturists, however, point to the absence of the word "church" (*ekklesia* in the Greek) after Revelation 3, claiming that the absence of that word supports the idea that the church is no longer on earth after Revelation 3. As already noted, they claim that the believers on earth spoken of in the book of Revelation after that point are Jews converted after the church has been caught up to heaven.

Doesn't it seem obvious, however, that the word "church" does not occur after Revelation 3 for the simple reason that John was no longer writing to seven existing churches and that he had shifted from a set of pastoral letters into a collection of apocalyptic visions, rather than because the church would be taken off the earth? Revelation itself does not explain the absence of the word "church" in that way. Such an assumption is an imposition on the text without valid justification from within the text. Nothing in what John wrote should lead us to fill in the blanks or add to the text in such a manner. We must always interpret the Word of God by the Word of God itself.

Further, John wrote in Revelation 1:1, "the things which must soon take place." "Soon" can only mean "soon." The letters to the seven churches could not therefore be about some distant future, but rather the realities of seven actual churches existing in John's day. These epistles have nothing to do with the end of a church age, the rapture of the saints, or any other related issue. The lessons and confrontations contained in them, however, can and should be applied to a multitude of similar situations in our own time. Further, John's assertion that these things must "soon" take place should lead us to root much of the rest of the book in events that actually happened in the first and second centuries, even though they may foreshadow other similar events in the distant future.

# Holy Spirit Withdrawn?

Let me reiterate something I said above. Many who take the view that the church will escape to heaven before the tribulation claim that the Holy Spirit will be withdrawn from the earth at the same time. The most glaring flaw in that argument, however, is revealed in First Corinthians 12:3: "Therefore I make known to you that no one speaking by the Spirit of God says, 'Jesus is accursed'; and no one can say, 'Jesus is Lord,' except by the Holy Spirit." Pretribulation proponents insist that the Jews will come to Jesus *en masse* after the church has been evacuated. If what the apostle Paul wrote about confessing Jesus as Lord is true, however, then how could anyone, no matter what their racial or religious heritage, confess Jesus as Lord if the Holy Spirit has been removed?

Often cited in support of the view that the Holy Spirit will be withdrawn is Second Thessalonians 2:7, "For the mystery of lawlessness is already at work; only he who now restrains will do so until he is taken out of the way." Note that the translators of the New American Standard Bible and many other versions fail to capitalize "he," indicating that the text does not justify identifying "he" as the Holy Spirit.

In truth, no one knows who or what Paul actually referred to. The most common speculation identifies "he" as the restraining influence that the Roman Empire, its army, and its legal system exercised upon the nations they dominated. Prior to the rise of the empire, the Mediterranean region had been a dangerous place for any kind of travel or commerce. The order and justice imposed by Rome all but eliminated brigands and pirates and made trade possible over the roads they built. The economy thrived as a result and the gospel traveled to the farthest reaches of the empire, enabled by what the Romans had established. When Rome fell, chaos and lawlessness reigned and the Dark Ages descended upon the Mediterranean and Europe.

## Would Jesus Allow His Bride to Suffer Through It?

People I respect have insisted that Jesus would never allow His beloved bride, the church, to go through a time of suffering like the Great Tribulation. Really? At the risk of sounding sarcastic, I think we might ask the more than 100,000 Christians martyred each year in modern times how they feel about that. Perhaps we should ask Middle Eastern Christians in Islamic states what they think. They are being driven from their homes, their churches are burned, and their bodies beheaded. Sounds like tribulation to me!

Did Jesus shield His bride from times of tribulation in Bible times? Absolutely not. Luke 21:36 says, "But keep on the alert at all times, praying that you may have strength to escape all these things that are about to take place, and to stand before the Son of Man." *Escape* in this context means strength to endure, to refuse to deny our Lord under pressure, rather than to evacuate. Jesus Himself said, "Because lawlessness is increased, most people's love will grow cold. But the one who endures to the end, he will be saved" (Matt. 24:12-13). Second Thessalonians 1:4 reads, "We ourselves speak proudly of you among the churches of God for your perseverance and faith in the midst of all your persecutions and afflictions which you endure." The hope of rapture and the kind of escape it implies requires no strength in the way that endurance and perseverance do. Our escape, our victory, is to have the power of perseverance to stand in the midst of tribulation rather than be defeated by it.

Let's look at Luke 21:36 in its actual historical context and the impact it would have had on the early church, more in keeping with the actual words spoken. Those who see prophecies of Scripture as applying only to the distant future will fail to put them in their historical and textual contexts. Jesus used the words, "about to take place," not as a reference to something to happen in the distant future. Further, the plural "you" to whom He spoke were the people standing before Him that day.

Prophetic perspective blends present, future, and distant future all into one frame. In this case, the entire chapter speaks to multiple time frames. What was "about to take place" in this layer of the blended frame was the Jewish rebellion against Rome and the utter destruction of the city and the temple with the loss of hundreds of thousands of lives. The church did, in fact, flee the city before its destruction and escaped what the rest of the population suffered. This particular part of the prophecy does not apply to the distant future and the actual end times.

So, whether Luke 21:36 is about us escaping by enduring, or is applicable only and specifically to the early church escaping the destruction of Jerusalem, it would seem to be abundantly clear that the rapture of the saints is not what Jesus had in mind.

As for whether or not Jesus would shield His bride from times of trial and tribulation, ask the apostle Paul. He wrote:

*Are they servants of Christ?—I speak as if insane—I more so; in far more labors, in far more imprisonments, beaten times without number, often in danger of death. Five times I received from the Jews thirty-nine lashes. Three times I was beaten with rods, once I was stoned, three times I was shipwrecked, a night and a day I have spent in the deep. I have been on frequent journeys, in dangers from rivers, dangers from robbers, dangers from my countrymen, dangers from the Gentiles, dangers in the city, dangers in the wilderness, dangers on the sea, dangers among false brethren; I have been in labor and hardship, through many sleepless nights, in hunger and thirst, often without food, in cold and exposure* (2 Corinthians 11:23-27).

Peter and the apostles were flogged. Herod had Peter imprisoned and intended to kill him after first executing James. The Jewish establishment stoned Stephen, the deacon, to death. Christians were fed to the lions in the Roman coliseum. Some were burned at the stake. Does it not seem that God has often allowed His people to undergo serious tribulations? These things have strengthened their witness. The sacrifices of martyrs in every age have never failed to bear fruit. "And they overcame him because of the blood of the Lamb and because of the word of their testimony, and they did not love their life even when faced with death" (Rev. 12:11). They "overcame." Victory!

## PREPARATION TO ENDURE

Finally, doesn't it seem that preparation to endure must be qualitatively different from preparation to escape? Doesn't the

Bible contain multiple exhortations to endure and to persevere in the face of trials? "You will be hated by all because of My name, but it is the one who has endured to the end who will be saved" (Matt. 10:22). And again, "But the one who endures to the end, he will be saved" (Matt. 24:13). The author of Hebrews understood this: "For consider Him who has endured such hostility by sinners against Himself, so that you will not grow weary and lose heart" (Heb. 12:3). James 1:12 declares, "Blessed is a man who perseveres under trial; for once he has been approved, he will receive the crown of life which the Lord has promised to those who love Him." It will be as if he had won a race and received the laurel wreath that served as a trophy in the ancient world.

Perhaps it was best stated by the apostle Paul in Romans 5:

> *And not only this, but we also exult in our tribulations, knowing that tribulation brings about perseverance; and perseverance, proven character; and proven character, hope; and hope does not disappoint, because the love of God has been poured out within our hearts through the Holy Spirit who was given to us* (Romans 5:3-5).

If I am preparing to escape and then find myself faced with the need to endure, am I not then in a weakened position? Unprepared, might I not then lose the battle? If, however, I am preparing to endure, and if I am doing what must be done to ready myself for the fiery trials I must face, and then I get to escape, what have I lost? Nothing! And I have gained strength, character, and hope in the process. We must prepare for our ultimate victory and refuse to buy into a defeatist theology that has us escaping a dying earth that we abandon to destruction.

# CHAPTER 6

# UNDERSTANDING THE REVELATION TO JOHN

IN THIS BOOK, I HAVE BEEN AND WILL BE UNPACKING VARI-ous elements of the Revelation to John. Here I give an overview to help the reader make simple sense of what can seem a complicated book.

John the apostle penned the Revelation from visions he received while exiled on the island of Patmos (off the east coast of Asia, now known as Turkey) in his old age sometime after A.D. 90. Assuming that Jesus called him as a disciple circa A.D. 30, we can assume he was between 80 and 90 years old. Apart from the letters to the seven churches in Revelation 2 and 3, it is apocalyptic literature written in symbolism needing interpretation.

Because of its symbolic and apocalyptic nature, no book of the Bible has caused more controversy or generated more confusion than the Revelation to John. To begin to understand, and to provide a grid for processing the information, please review my previous comments on the nature of apocalyptic literature.

Historically, the Book of Revelation and its symbols have been interpreted through the lenses of four different views. In other words, most of us read and understand almost any form of communication through a set of filters that determine how we perceive the content. Perceptions of the Book of Revelation are no exception. A summary of these four filters follows.

## FOUR DOMINANT VIEWS

### Preterist

Preterists believe that Revelation merely presents the events of the first century under the dominion of the Roman Empire, as well as the expectation the early church held of terrible persecution and the certainty that Jesus would return quickly to overthrow the Romans and rescue them. For pure preterists, everything contained in Revelation has already unfolded in the first century.

### Historical

People who see Revelation through this filter interpret the book as a symbolic record and prophecy of the entire history of the church from the first century down to the return of Jesus and the end of the age, which obviously has not yet occurred. This view divides the sections of the book into various periods of history in which God was and would be doing particular things through movements and trends.

### Idealist

To the idealist, Revelation is merely a symbolic representation of the cosmic conflict in the heavens between the powers of the kingdom of God and the powers of satanic evil. This can be reflected in events on earth but is not necessarily seen as a prophecy of coming earthly events.

### Futurist

Those who hold to this view read Revelation almost entirely as predictions of future events leading up to the end of the world, presented in symbolic terms. In the futurist view, which is usually adopted by adherents of Dispensationalism, the seven churches are seven successive periods of church history during the church age, while the remainder of the book is about the distant future leading directly to the end of the age.

# UNRAVELING THE CONFUSION

Historically, too much of the scholarship of the western world has sought to make the debate over these four views into a set of mutually exclusive understandings, as if only one way of seeing the Revelation to John can be acceptable. The truth is much more complex than that.

Several issues must be considered in order to achieve a balanced understanding. A foundational consideration must be that, as a man of his day and a product of his culture, John did not write in a historical or cultural vacuum. Revelation therefore contains reflections of actual first-century events and, in some cases, directly addresses them. Without an understanding of the cultural setting and history in which he lived, accurate understanding of what John wrote and saw becomes impossible. Preterism and the historical view therefore make some valid points.

A second issue involves the dynamic of "prophetic perspective," the way in which prophecy blends the present, the near future, and the distant future into one tapestry or one layered Photoshop frame. This means that some prophecies can have multiple fulfillments over time, many of them partial, before the final fullness unfolds. Futurism points to some truths in Revelation, but cannot be regarded as the whole truth.

Third, one would find it difficult to deny that the book contains elements of spiritual representations of heavenly events. Developments on earth do reflect spiritual realities. Thus, we must recognize the validity of some elements of the idealist view, while not taking it as the entire answer.

An intelligent blending of the core truths in each of these views therefore gives us the most accurate understanding.

# FOUNDATIONAL POINTS

John opened the Revelation in chapter 1, verse 1, by saying two significant things that must be remembered and accounted for. The first foundational point defines the book as, "The revelation of Jesus Christ." In other words, more than any other purpose, John intended to reveal the nature of Jesus in His essential divinity, His love, His power, and His sovereignty. Later on, in Revelation 19:10, this is underscored when John wrote, "For the testimony of Jesus is the spirit of prophecy." The key question is therefore not specifically what is supposed to happen, either in John's day or in the last days, but what do these things reveal about the nature, character, and identity of Jesus?

John knew that understanding the depth and reality of who Jesus is would equip the saints for the victories that lay ahead. Remember that he addressed the Revelation to real churches populated by real people facing real situations.

Second, John wrote that the content of the book would be, "the things which must soon take place," the key word being *soon*. In verse 3 he reinforced that assertion by saying, "the time is near." It simply won't do to defend a purely futurist view of Revelation in an attempt to explain away a delay of nearly two millennia by saying that to God a day is as a thousand years or that God's "soon" is not our "soon." Absent any textual indication of a different meaning, John meant "soon" in human terms, which means that much, though certainly not all, of the book of Revelation did, in fact, unfold in the years immediately following John's writing. In short, if the book is to be understood, it must be understood in the context of the period of time in which it was written.

# THE BASIC STRUCTURE

The heart of the book is made up of four sets of sevens—seven seals, seven trumpets, seven significant signs, and seven bowls of the wrath of God. Traditionally, these have been seen as consecutive periods of history, or segments of time, following one after the other, leading up to the return of Jesus. People ask, for instance, *Where do you think we are in the sequence? Are we into the seals, the trumpets, or the bowls?*

I want to suggest an alternate way of understanding these things that will make much more sense to most people. Suppose that you are watching a documentary movie of some significant event in history. Imagine that four different reporters filmed it from the perspectives of four different eyewitnesses to that event.

Suppose, for instance, that the subject is the Civil War in the United States, and specifically the turning point Battle of Gettysburg in Pennsylvania, July 1-3, 1863. One eyewitness might be a private in the infantry. Another might be one of the generals, while a third could be a doctor in the medical tent. A fourth could be a reporter for a newspaper surveying the battlefield from a safe vantage point.

Each of these would give an account of the same battle, each account accurate and true, but each would significantly differ from the others, depending on the perspective from which the reporter experienced and observed it. Reports on the depth and severity of the events witnessed would vary from person to person.

Told as a documentary film, the story would rewind to the beginning of the timeline after each sequence. The account would be presented again, beginning to end, but from a different angle, based on the vantage point and experience of the subject of that segment.

The same is true of the end-time accounts given in the Revelation to John. The core of it presents the same sequence of events, reported from four different perspectives, each leading up to the return of Jesus. Each successive perspective presents it perhaps more deeply than the one before but remains, nevertheless, the same story with the same ending. Seven is the number for completion, so each sequence of seven presents the completion of the end-time sequence of events, the Lord's return, and the end of the age.

### Seven Seals, Revelation 5:1–8:5

Picture a scroll rolled up and held closed along its length by seven wax seals so that it can be opened only when all seven seals have been broken. The scroll contains the written word of God with respect to the end of the age and the coming of the King. Seven seals and the events associated with the breaking of each seal tell us that this sequence presents the story of the end and the return of the Lord from the perspective of the opening and unfolding of the Word of God. This would have been of particular significance to the Jewish people who regarded the Scriptures as absolute reality and truth.

Now rewind the film's timeline to the beginning and roll it all again to tell the story from a fresh perspective.

### *Seven Trumpets, Revelation 8:6–9:19*

Begin by erasing from your mind the image of bright and shiny brass trumpets. Picture the *shofar,* or hollowed out ram's horn. In Bible times, such horns were used to communicate commands on the battlefield by means of certain patterns of blasts. More significantly for Revelation, the ram's horn announced important events or the coming of important persons. When the king approached, blasts of the *shofar* warned the people to prepare.

Seven trumpets and the events associated with each blast represent the telling of the end-time events leading up to, and culminating in, the return of Jesus from the perspective of the announcement of the coming of the King.

Once more, rewind the timeline to the beginning of the story to start it all again from yet another perspective.

### *Seven Significant Signs, Revelation 12:1–14:20*

John received seven visions of events in the cosmos, but the pattern is the same. Catastrophic events accelerate until the return of Jesus. The story in this case is told from the perspective of the effect of the return of the Lord upon the cosmos, or the heavenly representation of events on earth.

For the third time, reset the timeline to the beginning in order to tell it all again, this time from an even deeper perspective.

### *Seven Bowls of the Wrath of God, Revelation 16:1–21*

This one explains itself. The return of the Lord and the events leading up to it are portrayed in terms of God's wrath poured out on an unbelieving and sinful world. Once more it all culminates in the appearance of Jesus returning to establish His reign.

# The "Diamond" or "Jewel" View

If the idea of the same story told from different perspectives doesn't resonate for you, then think of it as the same light refracted through a crystal that breaks the light into its various colors. I call this "the diamond view" or "the jewel view." See the graphic:

**REVELATION TO JOHN**
JEWEL VIEW
One event refracted four ways.

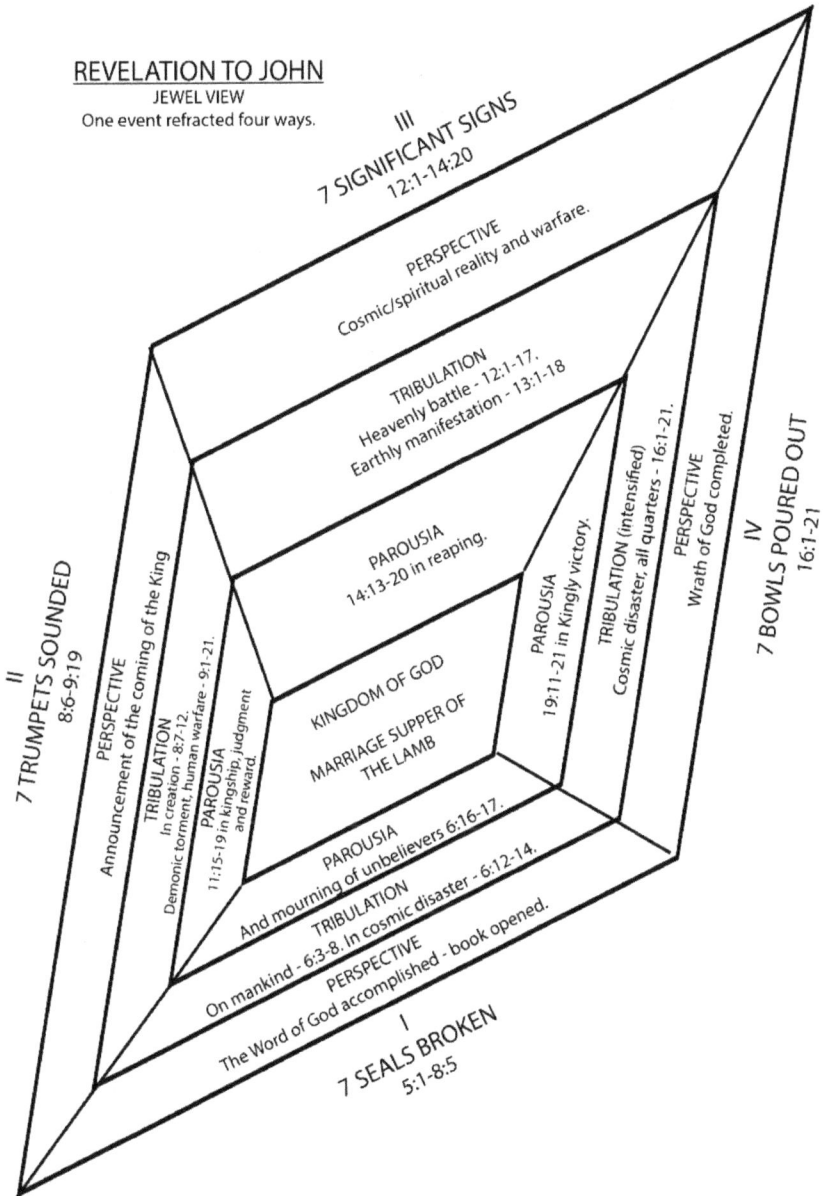

III
7 SIGNIFICANT SIGNS
12:1-14:20

PERSPECTIVE
Cosmic/spiritual reality and warfare.

TRIBULATION
Heavenly battle - 12:1-17.
Earthly manifestation - 13:1-18

PAROUSIA
14:13-20 in reaping.

KINGDOM OF GOD
MARRIAGE SUPPER OF THE LAMB

II
7 TRUMPETS SOUNDED
8:6-9:19

PERSPECTIVE
Announcement of the coming of the King

TRIBULATION
In creation - 8:7-12.
Demonic torment, human warfare - 9:1-21.

PAROUSIA
11:15-19 in kingship, judgment and reward.

IV
7 BOWLS POURED OUT
16:1-21

PERSPECTIVE
Wrath of God completed.

TRIBULATION (intensified)
Cosmic disaster, all quarters - 16:1-21.

PAROUSIA
19:11-21 in Kingly victory.

PAROUSIA
And mourning of unbelievers 6:16-17.

TRIBULATION
On mankind - 6:3-8. In cosmic disaster - 6:12-14.

PERSPECTIVE
The Word of God accomplished - book opened.

I
7 SEALS BROKEN
5:1-8:5

Obviously, this eliminates any thought of a pretribulation rapture of the church. In each sequence, the verses at the end clearly indicate the return of Jesus. The severity of the events increases from sequence to sequence because of the perspective from which each sequence is viewed. Referring again to my illustration of the various views of the Battle of Gettysburg, for instance, the account given by a reporter would be decidedly less traumatic than one told by an infantryman.

As the cycle of seals concludes, we read, "and they said to the mountains and to the rocks, 'Fall on us and hide us from the presence of Him who sits on the throne, and from the wrath of the Lamb; for the great day of their wrath has come, and who is able to stand?'" (Rev. 6:16-17). Jesus appears, and all those see Him in whom they have not previously believed. He has returned and people of the world become desperate to hide themselves from His consuming presence.

The trumpets have blown and it becomes immediately obvious that the story has once more been told from the beginning, but from yet another perspective. Once more it ends with the return of Jesus.

> *Then the seventh angel sounded; and there were loud voices in heaven, saying, "The kingdom of the world has become the kingdom of our Lord and of His Christ; and He will reign forever and ever." And the twenty-four elders, who sit on their thrones before God, fell on their faces and worshiped God, saying, "We give You thanks, O Lord God, the Almighty, who are and who were, because You have taken Your great power and have begun to reign. And the nations were enraged, and Your*

*wrath came, and the time came for the dead to be judged, and the time to reward Your bond-servants the prophets and the saints and those who fear Your name, the small and the great, and to destroy those who destroy the earth." And the temple of God which is in heaven was opened; and the ark of His covenant appeared in His temple, and there were flashes of lightning and sounds and peals of thunder and an earthquake and a great hailstorm* (Revelation 11:15-19).

Jesus has returned and taken up His throne.

Following the trumpets are seven significant signs. The account of the end-time events begins once more from the beginning, and then ends in the same place with the return of the Lord. "Then I looked, and behold, a white cloud, and sitting on the cloud was one like a son of man, having a golden crown on His head and a sharp sickle in His hand" (Rev. 14:14). Jesus identified Himself as the "the son of man" (see Matt. 8:20 and others). The crown and the term "the son of man" therefore confirm that the image is Jesus returning to earth at the end of the sequence. Verse 16 follows: "Then He who sat on the cloud swung His sickle over the earth, and the earth was reaped."

Finally, John retold the story from the perspective of God's wrath, beginning the account once more as the tribulation unfolds, and then concluding with the Lord's return. Just prior to pouring out the final bowl of the wrath of God, we see the Lord's return. "Behold, I am coming like a thief. Blessed is the one who stays awake and keeps his clothes, so that he will not walk about naked and men will not see his shame" (Rev. 16:15). At the appearance of the Lord, lightning flashes, thunder roars, and the greatest earthquake in the history of the world shakes the ground as God executes His full and final wrath.

None of these accounts of the Great Tribulation leading up to the return of the Lord can be said to include a rapture of the saints before the sequence begins. We don't escape. We endure, persevere, shine as lights in darkness, win others to the Lord, and, finally, we win.

CHAPTER 7

# VICTORY IN REVELATION

J OHN WROTE THE REVELATION TO ASSURE BELEAGUERED Christians of their ultimate victory and the glorious outcome. We find the book peppered, therefore, with images of believers standing in the glow of victory, having fought the good fight and prevailed.

> *And they sang a new song, saying, "Worthy are You to take the book and to break its seals; for You were slain, and purchased for God with Your blood men from every tribe and tongue and people and nation. You have made them to be a kingdom and priests to our God; and they will reign upon the earth"* (Revelation 5:9-10).

Key words: "they will reign upon the earth." At no point does Scripture present our destiny as escape to a non-corporeal existence in heaven. Ultimately, we reign with Jesus on a redeemed earth in resurrected bodies like His (see 1 Cor. 15). Originally addressed to Christians living under the oppression of the Roman Empire, Revelation assures persecuted believers that they will overcome whatever comes against them, and that they will reign, not in some bodiless state in heaven, but here on a redeemed earth. This is our destiny. Not escape. Not defeat. Not victims of a Great Tribulation from which we can only be delivered by means of the Lord's return. We reign now, even in the midst of opposition and oppression. Given our status as children of the King, why would we expect anything else?

We have been gifted to rule even when the world would see us as victims. The apostle Paul, under house arrest in Rome, nevertheless ministered to the Praetorian guard and spread the gospel through an entire unit of the Roman army. Polycarp, a disciple of John the apostle, while tied to the stake with flames leaping up to consume him, preached from the midst of the flames. The flames wouldn't touch him. Eyewitnesses spoke of a sweet aroma emanating from him. Unable to execute him by fire, the Romans finally ran a spear through him to silence his preaching. From the midst of the flames, he ruled. This is our heritage and our authority.

Whenever any strongman feels his control threatened, he fights back, whether or not he thinks he can win. Adolf Hitler, for instance, continued the fight until most of his capital city had been overrun by the Russians and bombs were shaking his underground bunker. Rather than give up easily, the devil will follow the same pattern, ramping up his attacks and fury until he meets his certain end. At the last, we will reign with Jesus, unopposed, on a redeemed earth, but we don't have to wait until the last day to rise above the circumstances of this world. Earthly kingdoms, no matter how strong or how evil, will never have the last word.

# THE 144,000

*And I saw another angel ascending from the rising of the sun, having the seal of the living God; and he cried out with a loud voice to the four angels to whom it was granted to harm the earth and the sea, saying, "Do not harm the earth or the sea or the trees until we have sealed the bond-servants of our God on their foreheads." And I heard the number of those who were sealed, one hundred and forty-four thousand sealed from every tribe of the sons of Israel (Revelation 7:2-4).*

While the earth around them suffers, the bond-servants of the Lord receive a seal on the forehead, marking them for protection in the midst of difficult times for the world and the demonic torment to come. Romans often branded their slaves on the foreheads to mark ownership. Those who know themselves to be fully given to the Lord, wholly owned by Him, will walk in victory in the midst of the destruction around them, having been marked and protected by His power and love.

In keeping with the nature of apocalyptic literature, the number 144,000 is best seen as entirely symbolic. First, the list of tribes in the following verses coincides with no other list of tribes in the Bible, which seems to indicate that this number does not represent literal Israel. Second, it would seem obvious that 12x12 = 144 represents twelve patriarchs and twelve apostles, fathers of the people of God under the Old Covenant together with fathers of the people of God under the New Covenant. In fact, 144 can be seen as a number representing governmental authority, which once more speaks of our victorious place in God's plan. We can then see the number 1,000 as representing an indeterminate large number of both Jews and Gentiles who have hoped in Jesus.

With the sounding of the fifth trumpet, demonic torment is loosed upon the earth to cause suffering to all those not included as part of the people of God represented in the 144,000 and who do not bear the seal. "They were told not to hurt the grass of the earth, nor any green thing, nor any tree, but only the men who do not have the seal of God on their foreheads" (Rev. 9:4). This seal of protection can hardly be seen as a rapture to escape the earth, but rather as an image of victory and preservation in the midst of judgments sent upon the unrighteous!

# INCENSE RISING

### *The Altar of Incense*

"When the Lamb broke the seventh seal, there was silence in heaven for about half an hour" (Rev. 8:1). While heaven awaits the blowing of the trumpets to announce the coming of the King, everything in heaven halts in breathless anticipation as God receives the prayers of the saints.

"And I saw the seven angels who stand before God, and seven trumpets were given to them" (Rev. 8:2). The trumpets announce the intervention of God in history, the return of the King, but the angels wait to sound them. They give time for the prayers of the saints to rise, offered up by the "holy ones" who have been cleansed and made pure by the blood of Jesus. They pause in anticipation of God's response to those prayers. Above all else, the sons and daughters of God soon to be revealed, the 144,000 wholly owned and sealed, are a praying people.

"Another angel came and stood at the altar, holding a golden censer; and much *incense was given to him, so that he might add it to the prayers of all the saints* on the golden altar which was before the throne. And the smoke of the incense, with the prayers of the saints, went up before God out of the angel's hand" (Rev. 8:3-4, emphasis mine). Prophetically speaking, I believe that we live now, quite literally, in the time of Revelation 8:3-4 when the prayers of the people of God mingle with the incense of heaven to be magnified before the throne of God. We live in a strategic period of history, the importance of which cannot be overemphasized. Many have sensed this. Thus we have seen the rise of 24/7 prayer centers around the world, spearheaded by the International House of Prayer and others.

John found himself witnessing a vision of the heavenly temple of which the earthly tabernacle of Moses and the temple in Jerusalem were mere pale reflections. According to the instructions given to Moses, the altar of incense stood immediately before the holy of holies where a curtain shielded the Ark of the Covenant, the earthly symbol of the very throne of God. Exodus 30:1 says, "Moreover, you shall make an altar as a place for burning incense; you shall make it of acacia wood." Incense symbolizes prayer rising to the Lord as a pleasing aroma to Him. "Its length shall be a cubit, and its width a cubit, it shall be square, and its height shall be two cubits; its horns shall be of one piece with it" (Exod. 30:2). By our modern measurement, the altar of incense stood approximately three feet high and a foot and a half square, or approximately a meter high and half a meter square. While a horn-shaped decoration accented each corner, a low railing around the top prevented the incense and ashes from falling out.

God instructed Moses to overlay this altar with gold and to equip it with rings and poles for transport. He then continued: "You shall put this altar in front of the veil that is near the ark of the testimony, in front of the mercy seat that is over the ark of the testimony, where I will meet with you" (Exod. 30:6). The ark of the testimony symbolized His presence. Through prayer, we encounter that presence. This entire scene implies intimate prayer in the immediate presence of God. We live now in a strategic kingdom season of victory that calls for intensified and urgent prayer in preparation for both the glory and the troubles to come as the time of the Lord's return approaches.

"You shall not offer any strange incense on this altar, or burnt offering or meal offering; and you shall not pour out a drink offering on it" (Exod. 30:9). Incense for the altar of incense was made according to a particular formula forbidden to be used anywhere else. No other kind of incense made from any other formula could legally be burned on that altar.

During this season of the interlude prior to the re-telling of the sequence of events leading to the Lord's return, we must therefore pray in the manner God commands us, according to His will and in tune with His wishes. Understanding His heart, we must pray in harmony with His heart. Otherwise, our offering of incense will be offensive and inappropriate, improperly formulated. Prayer in this season must not be centered on us, our personal needs, or our individual desires. That's not to say that we can't pray for personal needs. At issue is our overall focus. Because no prayer, even of a personal nature, other than that which reflects His heart and His desires will be heard or accepted during this strategic time when intimacy with God and death of self carry a heightened level of urgency. One often-missed reason for God's desire to revive and refine the prophetic movement is that prophetic people bear a calling to discern the heart of God and inform the body of Christ how to pray accordingly.

"Aaron shall make atonement on its horns once a year; he shall make atonement on it with the blood of the sin offering of atonement once a year throughout your generations. It is most holy to the Lord" (Exod. 30:10). From time to time, repentance and forgiveness were included in the prayers in order to keep them pure. Praying like that seen in Revelation 8 must therefore include elements of cleansing, times of deep repentance, and heartfelt brokenness. The contemporary church desperately and urgently needs a movement of repentance and brokenness, especially if we expect to be effective in intercession during this strategic period of history. Let those of us who understand the importance of holiness cry out for it. Without repentance and brokenness we cannot come to wholeness, and without wholeness the sons and daughters of God can never be formed and revealed.

## The Nature of Our Prayers

"Then the angel took the censer and filled it with the fire of the altar, and threw it to the earth; and there followed peals of thunder and sounds and flashes of lightning and an earthquake" (Rev. 8:5). In response to the prayers of the saints rising with the incense of heaven, the angel casts fire from the altar of incense into the earth. In the last days, this season of our victory, heaven magnifies our prayers, increasing the power of the prayers of the saints offered on earth.

Many commentators see this fire cast into the earth as God's vengeance and judgment upon the ungodly and those who persecute believers. They believe that the prayers of the saints in Revelation 8:2-5 petition God to send punishment upon those who harmed them. Jesus, however, called us to love our enemies and to bless and pray for them. Neither vengeance nor hatred flow from the Spirit we have been given. Yes, God will eventually execute judgement on those who harm His people, but this is not the place for that. For this to be the fire of judgment would contradict everything the Lord taught us concerning our role on earth.

As I have so often stated, John first wrote Revelation to reassure and equip believers suffering persecution under Roman domination. Because he set the Revelation against the backdrop of the experience of the people to whom he wrote, much of it applies only indirectly to the future. We then draw lessons for life today from what has already taken place in history. The early Christians under persecution eventually converted the Roman Empire by leading untold thousands of people to Jesus because believers became so known for their sacrificial love for any and all people that in A.D. 314 the emperor Constantine declared himself and the entire empire to be Christian.

Taken together, history and the teaching of Jesus tell us that these prayers in Revelation 8 must not be interpreted as petitions for vengeance or judgment. Likewise, the fire cast into the earth in response to these prayers must not be seen as the fire of destruction, but rather the "fire of the altar," prayer fire, fire sent from heaven in response to prayer, fire that energizes prayer, and fire flowing from the kind of intimacy with God that the altar of incense represents.

Thus, in our day, we see movements of prayer springing up around the world. People with a heart for prayer are hearing the call of God, understanding the urgency of the hour, and are responding to lay the foundation for a resounding end-time victory. We live literally in the time John foresaw and recorded in the first few verses of Revelation 8.

## THE SYMBOLISM OF FIRE

### In the Old Testament

Fire in the Old Testament often indicated that God had accepted or received a sacrifice, as when Elijah confronted the 450 prophets of Baal and challenged them to call fire from heaven (see 1 Kings 18). All day they danced around and cut themselves, shedding their blood to no avail. Elijah then built an altar of stones, placed the sacrifice upon it, poured water on all of it three times, and then cried out to God. As God received the offering, fire fell from heaven to consume the sacrifice, the altar, and even the stones.

This fire in Revelation therefore tells us that, during this season prior to the sequence of events leading to the end, God hears and receives the prayers of the saints and honors their sacrifices. The angel adding the incense of heaven to it indicates that our prayers are magnified in power as they rise to God. During this period in which we now live, heaven empowers our prayers for the kingdom of God to be manifest on earth. In the fire sent in response to those prayers, our victory unfolds. Light rises in darkness for us, the upright.

Fire fell from heaven at the consecration of Solomon's Temple.

Fire describes God's glory (see Dan. 7:9), symbolizes His holiness (see Isa. 33:14), and stands for His protection over His people (see 2 Kings 6:17; Zech. 2:5)

First and foremost, in Old Testament times, fire represented God Himself. He revealed Himself to Moses in the burning bush. When He showed Himself among the Hebrew people in the desert, He guided them with fire by night and smoke by day.

### In the New Testament

When the disciples asked if Jesus would allow them to call for fire from heaven to consume those in Samaria who would not receive Jesus, He replied, "You do not know what kind of spirit you are of" (Luke 9:55). In the Lord's Prayer, He taught us to pray for the kingdom of God to come on earth, for His presence to be manifest, and for His will to be carried out here. "Your kingdom come. Your will be done, on earth as it is in heaven" (Matt. 6:10). The fire cast into the earth in response to prayer in Revelation 8 must therefore be understood as the fire of His presence and anointing, the manifestation of the kingdom of God. We live in a day of acceleration and intensification in kingdom things. Signs and wonders proliferate as expressions of His love in keeping with the rule of the kingdom of God.

> *As for me, I baptize you with water for repentance, but He who is coming after me is mightier than I, and I am not fit to remove His sandals; He will baptize you with the Holy Spirit and fire* (Matthew 3:11).

> *I have come to cast fire upon the earth; and how I wish it were already kindled!* (Luke 12:49)

> *And there appeared to them tongues as of fire distributing themselves, and they rested on each one of them. And they were all filled with the Holy Spirit and began to speak with other tongues, as the Spirit was giving them utterance* (Acts 2:3-4).

> *And when He again brings the firstborn into the world, He says, "And let all the angels of God worship Him." And of the angels He says, "Who makes His angels winds, and His ministers a flame of fire"* (Hebrews 1:6-7).

"Therefore, since we receive a kingdom which cannot be shaken, let us show gratitude, by which we may offer to God an acceptable service with reverence and awe; for our God is a consuming fire" (Heb. 12:28-29). We receive a kingdom from the One who is a consuming fire.

The fire cast into the earth in answer to the prayers of the saints in Revelation must therefore be fire such as fell on the day of Pentecost, visibly witnessed as flames on their heads, when 3,000 men with their families came to Jesus. This fire burns in us who receive it in order to carry us beyond ourselves into the world to set others aflame in this strategic time. By the mercy of God, this flame from heaven saves lives and heals the broken. This is kingdom fire representing the greatest outpouring of the Spirit of God since the day of Pentecost. It is the fire and fuel of victory for those who choose to receive it. Before Jesus returns, we get to win.

## SUMMARY AND APPLICATION

We stand on the threshold of the last days during the interval in time just before the angels blow the seven trumpets that announce the sequence of events leading to the Lord's return. It is a time for strategic prayer in a strategic season, a time when our prayers will be amplified by the very angels of heaven to empower our victory. In the days to come, expect an escalating sense of urgency, power, and presence on prayer meetings that once perhaps seemed lifeless, routine, or boring. If you don't feel that urgency emotionally, then choose it, because the urgency remains regardless of human emotion.

Prayer in this crucial period of time and beyond will be unlike anything we have ever known as the angel adds heavenly incense to it. Heaven will answer with kingdom fire from the heavenly altar of God. This fire of the kingdom of God will ignite more than just miracles, healings, deliverance, or even raising the dead. It will result in more than merely winning people to Jesus. This fire is the will of heaven come to earth. "Your kingdom come. Your will be done, on earth as it is in heaven" (Matt. 6:10). We get to carry out that will in His name.

# CHAPTER 8

# THE REVEALING OF THE SONS OF GOD

At a time when much of the church has been seduced by a doctrine of cheap and easy grace, one must ask whether holiness still matters. In these last days, it certainly does. But what does it mean? What is required? Let me begin by saying that holiness never begins with outward behavior working to bring inner change. Rather, it begins with a change of heart and character working to determine behavior. It can never be performed, only imparted, received, and expressed, but never achieved by performance. We act in holiness because we've been made holy by the One who is holy.

## ROMANS 8:19: THE REVEALING OF THE SONS OF GOD

*For the anxious longing of the creation waits eagerly for the revealing of the sons of God.*

Jewish people living in the Middle East, whose first language was most often Aramaic (a form of Hebrew), wrote our New Testament in Greek. They did so because Greek had become the common language of the Roman Empire, much as English in our own day has become so commonly spoken and understood around the world. They wanted to reach as many people as possible. Under Aramaic influence, Hebrew forms of expression made their way into the manner in which the writers expressed the Greek, especially when it came to descriptions of people. For instance, when the Gospel of Mark referred to James and John, the description in Mark 3:17 was "sons of thunder." This identified them as thunderous men whose personalities were probably loud and strong. Similarly, in Ephesians 2:2 those whose lives are characterized by sin are called "sons of disobedience."

The Hebrew expression "sons of God" therefore describes those whose natures have been visibly "conformed to the image of His Son" (Rom. 8:29). The apostle wrote of a generation of believers, both men and women, to emerge in the last days whose character could be said to have been substantially transformed and conformed to the image of Jesus. I call it holiness. The world would come to know who Jesus truly is simply by coming to know this generation of believers in their love, their mercy, their integrity, and the sense of the presence of God upon them. In spite of the popularity and impact of the hyper-grace message that seems too often to lower the bar for morality and behavior, holiness still matters, especially in these last days and in light of our appointed victory. I believe this end-time generation is about to emerge, not as an elite cadre of super-Christians, but as a generation, perhaps a remnant, who truly understand and walk in the heart of the Father.

I believe that Paul wrote of an emerging group of people who refuse compromise and who diligently seek holiness and wholeness, not for selfish reasons, personal happiness, or prosperity, but for the sake of loving the Lord and people more purely, restfully, and with greater effect. Who they are and how they live will reveal to the world what our God is truly like. Having been substantially changed to conform to the image of Jesus, they radiate a heart of love to think, feel, and act as Jesus in the power of the Holy Spirit and through character that has been refined and cleansed by embracing His cross and His blood. Galatians 2:20 rings true for them: "I have been crucified with Christ; and it is no longer I who live, but Christ lives in me; and the life which I now live in the flesh I live by faith in the Son of God, who loved me and gave Himself up for me."

Where victory for this generation is concerned, godly character prevails and shines in a dark and lawless world to manifest the nature of our God. Even from the most hardened unbelievers, character garners respect. With respect comes credibility and favor, just as it did for Joseph under Pharaoh and for Daniel as he served Nebuchadnezzar. Under different names and in various ways, this same group shows up more than once in Scripture.

# REVELATION 14: THE 144,000 (AGAIN)

The fourteenth chapter of Revelation contrasts the destinies of two disparate groups of people. This differentiation existed in the Roman Empire in John's day and it manifests now with a quality of end-time urgency. In keeping with prophetic perspective, the first century saw this contrast foreshadowed, but I believe it will soon manifest in fullness in our day. This calls for decision on the part of every person who believes in the name of Jesus. Where will you stand? With which group will you identify? Will you settle for less, or press forward for the fullness of what our Lord has to offer? That fullness enriches every aspect of life from family and personal relationships to an overall sense of purpose. Love in its purest expression changes everything.

Remember that Revelation is apocalyptic literature employing fluid symbolism like that found in dreams. Much as you and I might have dreams filled with symbolism, John saw prophetic visions, pregnant with meaning but full of symbolism needing interpretation. This applies to the 144,000 of whom John wrote.

Revelation 14:1 says, "Then I looked, and behold, the Lamb was standing on Mount Zion, and with Him one hundred and forty-four thousand, having His name and the name of His Father written on their foreheads." As has already been pointed out, we find the whole composition of the body of Christ represented in the number 144,000—Jews and Gentiles who believe in Jesus, twelve patriarchs times twelve apostles. The number 1,000 is simply a way of saying "a great many."

One key argument against taking this as a literal number is that in taking it literally, according to verse 4, these must all be men not "defiled with women"—sorry ladies! You're excluded! More on that in a moment! For now, understand that this number includes Jew and Gentile, male and female, all those who have received Jesus as Lord, Messiah, and Savior and who have determined to follow Him fully. As already noted, this group appears first in Revelation 7:3-4 where they were sealed against the plagues to come.

To mark ownership, Romans often branded slaves on the forehead. Their foreheads bear the names of Jesus and the Father God. Symbolically represented in terms first-century Christians would understand, the 144,000 have given themselves as "slaves" of Jesus and the Father. Doesn't that sound like the Romans 8:19 sons of God to be revealed in the last days, looking like Jesus, wholly owned and completely sold out to Him? These are neither the compromisers nor those who claim the name but fail to walk the walk. These "slaves" have surrendered their freedoms for the greater freedom to be found in Jesus. Slaves to Jesus know that full obedience to Him is the only true freedom and that everything else constitutes actual slavery.

"Standing on Mount Zion" the place where God chose to manifest His presence indicates that these live and move in the presence of God, that He has chosen to dwell in their midst, and that they love nothing more than His presence. There is no compelling reason to believe that John saw a literal 144,000, men only, all concentrated on the hill of Zion. Mount Zion in the Old Testament was the place where God chose to make His name to dwell. As the place of His presence, it therefore symbolizes His presence wherever He might choose to manifest it.

So, these 144,000 walk, stand, and live in God's raw and imminent presence. As a focused and singular goal, they have sought intimacy with Him and have been changed by their experience of it. The tangible sense of God's nearness has become their home wherever they go. In these last days, this is the destiny of all those who make the choice to follow Jesus without reservation, both men and women. In light of this, perhaps the important question is not *when will Jesus return* but rather *are we being transformed into the image of our Lord in the Father's heart?* Have we been seeking to know when Jesus will return to take us away when we should have been hungering for His transforming presence to invade us here and now? Ask the wrong question and you will likely get the wrong answer.

## PURCHASED FROM THE EARTH

Revelation 14:3 says the 144,000 have been "purchased from the earth." No longer citizens of earth, bought by the blood of the Lamb, they have been marked on the forehead as belonging to Him. A slave is owned. Purchased. The price of the purchase was the blood of the Lamb. We are not our own. We have no rights except the right to become children of God (see John 1:12). This is the slavery whose true name is freedom.

Revelation 14:4-5 reads, "These are the ones who have not been defiled with women, for they have kept themselves chaste. These are the ones who follow the Lamb wherever He goes. These have been purchased from among men as first fruits to God and to the Lamb. And no lie was found in their mouth; they are blameless."

Women are certainly not defiling and there is nothing defiling about sex within the confines of marital relationships. Jesus consistently treated women with honor and saw them as a source of blessing. In fact, in a time when women were not allowed to study the Torah and were kept apart from the men behind a veil in the synagogue, Jesus included women among the disciples who sat at His feet. This was revolutionary! Scripture calls for men to treat women with that same quality of respect. These verses are not therefore about women. We find here yet another reason not to view the 144,000 as a literal number or to regard the imagery as anything but symbolic of a spiritual reality. What then does this actually imply?

The answer can be found in Israel's history of idolatry. "Defiled with women" is a biblical metaphor for compromised devotion to God. Jeremiah 3:8-9 reads, "And I saw that for all the adulteries of faithless Israel, I had sent her away and given her a writ of divorce, yet her treacherous sister Judah did not fear; but she went and was a harlot also. Because of the lightness of her harlotry, she polluted the land and committed adultery with stones and trees." As the prophets confronted Israel's sins of idolatry, sexual immorality became a paradigm for Israel's unfaithfulness to God through the worship of other gods.

Harlotry—a strong word! God labeled faithless Israel a bunch of whores engaged in betrayal of their Husband. A whore gets paid for her services. Similarly, the fertility gods Israel whored after offered payment for their services in the form of crops and flocks. Sin offers a reward, a payment, but it's a lie. Compromise with sin brings defilement, destroying both glory and blessing in the same way as does sexual immorality. In sin, you join the culture around you and buy into its values and attitudes for the sake of a reward that's actually delusion and defilement.

Jeremiah 5:7 makes a similar point: "Why should I pardon you? Your sons have forsaken Me and sworn by those who are not gods. When I had fed them to the full, they committed adultery and trooped to the harlot's house." God was saying, *You experienced Me and my goodness but traded it for defilement and loss.*

Yet again in Ezekiel 23:43-44, naming the northern and southern kingdoms of Israel, God said, "Then I said concerning her who was worn out by adulteries, 'Will they now commit adultery with her when she is thus?' But they went in to her as they would go in to a harlot. Thus they went in to Oholah and to Oholibah, the lewd women." Compromise with the deceptions of the Baal spirit brings the strongest of condemnations. We are His bride. He expects fidelity and has every right to do so.

The 144,000, the faithful bride of Christ, refuse any form of compromise with the godless world system of religion and philosophy. Firmly committed to Jesus and to Jesus alone, they remain absolutely moral in every way there is to be moral. Their devotion is pure.

This end-time company of sons and daughters of God "follow the Lamb wherever He goes." A symbolic way of speaking of absolute obedience, this willingness to follow defines a key element of their chastity, much like the first twelve disciples who left everything to follow Jesus without condition, not knowing where they were going. The obedient heart follows, even when it cannot see the road ahead.

## FIRST FRUITS

John saw the 144,000 as "first fruits" purchased from among the people of the world. In agricultural terms, first fruits guarantee the full harvest to come. In the verses that follow, John wrote that the world will rush headlong into a time when every aspect of the ungodly world system will collapse. In the midst of this collapse, as people experientially discover that sin doesn't work, and as pain and destruction drive people to despair, we will see a great end-time harvest of souls, even as the majority fail to repent. This end-time company of Jews and Gentiles devoted to Jesus is merely the vanguard of a great harvest of souls to come in the last days. Victory unfolds at every point.

## A PEOPLE OF ABSOLUTE INTEGRITY

John wrote that this end-time company of sold-out believers would be a people of absolute integrity, "And no lie was found in their mouth; they are blameless" (Rev. 14:5). Aren't you tired of reading and hearing reports of prominent Christian leaders fallen to sin and compromise? While in New Zealand speaking for a conference, I heard from my hosts eyewitness accounts of pastors from foreign countries attending the Lakeland Revival in Lakeland, Florida (circa 2008) who bought expensive items from stores where they talked the clerks into writing up false invoices so that they would not have to pay as much in duties upon leaving the country. Sadly, this kind of unrighteousness has been all too common. In these last days, holiness counts, perhaps as never before!

In the days to come, no level of compromise will do. Lapses of integrity and morality will disqualify us to be included among the revealed sons of God walking with the Lord in intimacy, glory, and victory. Such failures of holiness will prevent us entering into the depth of the new worship represented in the "new song" and will disqualify us to be included as among the first fruits. We are called as world-changers who walk in victory and authority, but we cannot do it from positions of compromise. In the days to come, holiness will be wedded with the power and authority of the kingdom of God manifest on earth. Power like we have never seen will be released. Know that I am not saying we must all be perfect. Not possible! I am, however, pointing out the necessity of desiring and pursuing deep godliness of character in these last days.

As a full-time pastor for forty-two years at this writing, I grieve as I have seen too many believers waiting until the last minute to put their lives in order. One might wonder—what level of delusion would lead us to believe that life in the world is worth delaying life in the glory? Do we not understand that to continue in ungodly ways without repentance means that we are storing up destruction for ourselves?

If you knew that you could collect a million dollars tomorrow if you simply gave up eating sugar, would you put off denying yourself those donuts until next month? Would you reach for a candy bar? Why wait? Sin kills. Light fades, for instance, from the eyes of fornicators when freedom and glory could be had now, today, by choosing righteousness. Refusal to forgive destroys love at every level of life, even for those we most want to love. In short, any transgression of any one of the basic Ten Commandments destroys something of our essential humanity, and yet sin continues to appeal. God calls the compromisers "whores" because the initial payment for illicit sin is the delusory and temporary pleasure we get from doing it, although the end is destruction and loss. We get to win, but we can only do it by growing in conformity to the image of Jesus.

Review once more Romans 8:19, "For the anxious longing of the creation waits eagerly for the revealing of the sons of God," and Romans 8:29-30, "For those whom He foreknew, He also predestined to become conformed to the image of His Son, so that He would be the firstborn among many brethren; and these whom He predestined, He also called; and these whom He called, He also justified; and these whom He justified, He also glorified." Clearly Revelation 14 is John's vision of the same group of people Paul foresaw in Romans 8.

In any case, all of this points to another aspect of the victory promised us as we approach the time of the end.

CHAPTER 9

# WORSHIP IN THE LAST DAYS

*And I heard a voice from heaven, like the sound*
*of many waters and like the sound of loud*
*thunder, and the voice which I heard was like*
*the sound of harpists playing on their harps.*
*And they sang a new song before the throne*
*and before the four living creatures and the*
*elders; and no one could learn the song except*
*the one hundred and forty-four thousand*
*who had been purchased from the earth.*
—REVELATION 14:2-3

# WORSHIP BY THE "SONS OF GOD" IN THE LAST DAYS

Fluid imagery like that of dreams and visions marks the language of Revelation. Here, for instance, John spoke of a sound both thunderously loud like that of a large waterfall, yet delicate as the plucking of a chorus of harps, both overpowering and gentle, forceful and soft, shaking and comforting. John heard the glorious sound of the voices of a multitude rising as one, the resonant wonder of worship offered in the power of kingdom unity.

I believe this generation of worshipers lives now and that they stand in the vanguard of a movement of worship reflecting God's nature, infused with all the qualities of His presence. The sons of God to be manifest in the last days stand above all as a worshiping people. The last days outpouring of the Holy Spirit will spark a wondrous revival of heavenly worship on earth.

This worship revival rejects the entertainment model focused on the performance of those on the stage as if worship were a concert. In these last days, worship among the wholly owned, symbolized by the 144,000, will grow in power as well as the gentle touch, the roar as well as the whisper, and thunderous proclamation as well as sweet comfort. Already begun, this new pulse of worship can flow only from the hearts of the sold-out, one hundred percent laid-down lovers of God. As a "sound from heaven" this worship originates in the realm of the Spirit and manifests on earth.

John wrote, "And they sang a new song before the throne and before the four living creatures and the elders; and no one could learn the song except the one hundred and forty-four thousand who had been purchased from the earth" (Rev. 14:3).

As worship takes on a growing force and power among the sons and daughters of God in these last days—our day—it will be characterized by a sense of intensity and urgency, as well as exhibiting a quality of unique creativity.

Implied in these verses is the idea that not everyone can enter into this new depth of worship and in effect "learn" it because it can only be truly felt and offered up by those who have been branded as wholly owned. It flows from a place in the heart that has been profoundly touched and changed, a place that has come to look a lot like Jesus so that it resonates powerfully with His Spirit.

A worship revival is being released in these last days to energize the spirit of our victory in Jesus, a "song" that comes exclusively from undivided hearts hopelessly in love with our Lord. The compromisers and the lukewarm cannot learn the depth of it because it requires wholeness of devotion. Others will hear it who have not come into that kind of relationship with Jesus. They will sense it and be drawn by the supernatural presence of God in it, but will not be able to comprehend its depth or the fullness of its power without making the same decision the laid-down lovers have made. This worship revival has already begun for those who can learn the song. The invitation to make the choices that lead to the fullness of this precious gift has gone out. The only question is, who will respond?

I believe that as this new wave of worship washes over those able to learn the song and enter in, we will see a dramatic increase of sovereign signs and wonders poured out in the context of worship. Worship will move from being simply collections of musicians playing songs and will become a glorious act of surrender led by prophetic psalmists. Prophetic words will be sung from the heart of God. In the midst of worship, words of knowledge will come forth concerning what God is doing among the people at that moment, and power will be released.

In First Chronicles 25 David and the commanders of his army appointed skillful musicians and singers to prophesy on their instruments and with their voices. God intended that worship should carry not just the glory of God, but a military benefit. Perhaps more significantly, Heman, the king's seer, a prophet, exercised authority over the whole. From the Old Testament to the New Testament, God intended worship to be both prophetic and strategic for victory. Later, when Solomon dedicated the temple built with the materials David had prepared, such a glory cloud descended in response to the sacrifices offered that the priests could not stand to minister. God hasn't changed.

Obviously, this kind of worship revival with a prophetic empowering cannot happen where the movement of the Holy Spirit is restricted or forbidden. Look for manifestations of this kind in what I call "lighthouse churches" where extended worship, pursued to breakthrough into the Presence, is practiced and cherished. Increasingly, God will move in healing power in the context of worship without the mediation of any human agent or gifted superstar leader. Already, in some places, this has begun to manifest. My own church has seen a number of people healed in this sovereign manner during the course of powerful worship when no one was praying for them. It's all part of the "new song" and it doesn't require a superstar healer on the platform making it all happen and doing it all *for* us.

How does this work? What does it look like? As a worship leader, I am not only engaged in worshiping and leading the band. I'm listening to God, asking Him what He is doing, as well as sensing in my spirit what the people are feeling and doing. Without breaking rhythm or exiting whatever song we might be singing, I will simply announce or even sing the thing I'm hearing.

For instance, one brother in our flock had suffered from severe ulcers for fifteen years. During worship, I sensed a healing anointing in the room. While continuing to play the chords of the song, I invited people to notice any bodily sensations and choose to receive them as the hand of God. This brother felt the touch of God flood his body. Scheduled for surgery the following week, he went for a pre-surgery gastroscopy. The result? Where there had been scar tissue evident in previous examinations, there was now no evidence that he had ever had an ulcer.

In another case, a brother, functionally blind in one eye due to diabetic complications, felt the sovereign touch of God during one of our services. God restored his eye to 20/20 vision, better than it had been before losing his sight. The doctors had offered him little to no hope of recovery. Other healings have happened in our midst when I as a worship leader was completely unaware. Sovereign acts of our loving God will increase as His presence is welcomed.

In short, in this coming season the office of the prophet will be wedded with the office of the psalmist. God will speak and God will heal in the context of worship offered up as much more than merely the warmup to the sermon. Worship and the preaching of the Word will occupy equal places of importance.

Creativity will be released in both spontaneous song and in fresh songs for worship that comprise the new hymns of our day, contemporary in style and filled with rich poetic content. A vanguard of creative and original songwriters already move in this renewed anointing.

Once more, however, I must make it clear that this surge of freshly anointed worship will not fully touch the lukewarm or unclean of heart except where they allow it to incite deeper passion for the Lord. Sovereign signs and wonders like this will not be seen in churches where the move of God is limited and where lukewarm and less than radical commitment is tolerated in the name of not wanting to alienate anyone. To borrow a phrase from Jesus's own language, "the time is coming and now is," when nothing less than radical commitment and the kind of extended and passionate worship that brings the Presence will be enough to satisfy the needs of those crying out for help in a desperate time.

I believe that we are the generation John foresaw. Now. Today. We must pursue a depth of worship that exhibits all the qualities of God, reflecting who He is. It is not entertainment. It's a mirror of God Himself and it strengthens us for victory even as it glorifies the Lord.

# CHAPTER 10

# THE LAST DAYS
# HARVEST

*And I saw another angel flying in midheaven,
having an eternal gospel to preach to those
who live on the earth, and to every nation
and tribe and tongue and people; and he said
with a loud voice, "Fear God, and give Him
glory, because the hour of His judgment has
come; worship Him who made the heaven and
the earth and sea and springs of waters."*

—REVELATION 14:6-7

In Revelation 14:6-7, I see shades of Matthew 24:14: "This gospel of the kingdom shall be preached in the whole world as a testimony to all the nations, and then the end will come." Here we read and hear the final call prior to the Lord's return as we come near to achieving the goal of reaching every tribe, tongue, and nation. As we approach the season of the last chance, no time remains for playing games. John foresaw a supernaturally empowered push in the last days to save as many as possible before the Lord's return. Even as judgment falls upon the world and its ungodly systems, a great victorious ingathering will be underway.

Obviously, in light of this, we must wake up and get serious about being followers of our Lord and Father. As we transition into the time of the greater vision of the kingdom of God beyond ourselves, we must leave behind the old season when so much of Christian teaching focused on solving our personal problems and enter a time of victorious impact on the world around us. Our Lord will always be about personal healing and blessing, but self-focus leads inevitably to defeat.

## HISTORY AND FORESHADOWING

Christians in John's day stood their ground and responded in love to vicious persecution. They were the symbolic 144,000 of the first and second centuries who foreshadowed the fullness of the coming of the wholly owned in the last days. The gospel went forth in power and love in the early years of the church and drew people from every nation, tribe, and tongue in the Roman Empire. In keeping with the dynamic of prophetic perspective, John saw this harvest realized in his own time, but what the Lord revealed to him clearly pointed to something larger, yet to unfold. Before the Lord's return, a more significant 144,000 would be called and revealed. By and through the 144,000 of the last days, a larger harvest of souls would be won. I believe those days are upon us.

## THE ANGEL FLYING IN MIDHEAVEN

In the Revelation to John, events on earth are often reflected in the heavens. In this case, heaven actually initiates events on earth as the angel releases the word of the gospel. A calling, with anointing to fulfill it, now goes forth to proclaim throughout the earth that Jesus is Lord, that He has saved us by His sacrifice, and that He has risen from the dead as the first fruits of those of us who follow Him. An invitation sounds forth, summoning people to come and worship Him. Supernaturally empowered, this call resounds from heaven and impacts those who can hear it on earth. Paradoxically, this call for redemption sounds from heaven at the same time as judgment and destruction manifest on earth.

## THE CHALLENGE

This challenge may apply mostly to western culture, but the lesson can be applied wherever appropriate. Recent decades have seen an emphasis on ministry beyond the walls of the church, in the marketplace, on the streets, and in neighborhoods. Those gifted with the necessary boldness take joy in approaching strangers, coworkers, and acquaintances with offers of prayer for healing, prophetic words, and more. Some churches and groups have trained and deployed teams to interpret dreams in coffeehouses and other settings. In my own church I've trained and deployed a team to interpret dreams at places like Starbucks. All it takes is to purchase a cup or two, place a small sign on the table saying "Free Dream Interpretation" and people come. In addition to dream interpretation, all kinds of ministry flows from this, from prayer for relational issues to prayer for healing. People are both hungry and receptive.

Not long ago, such things would have been rejected by most, perceived even as threatening. "Can I pray for you?" would have been met with a firm answer of, "No!" but no longer. A shift has happened. Where once the answer was, "No!" the response is now, "Oh yes! Please!" In the midst of an increasingly uncertain world, somewhere deep in the hearts of a growing number of people a longing for something transcendent has taken root. As we witness the accelerating collapse of a once great society, the disintegration of the family, international turmoil, confusion over sexual identity, proliferation of substance abuse and more, an undercurrent of fear and apprehension grows and is felt even by the least sensitive among us.

Obviously, this is fertile soil for those of us who shine with the Spirit of the living God. People are being touched and ministered to. The challenge? Every seed must be watered and fertilized. Every harvest must be gathered into the barn. Every newly born child needs a family in order to grow into healthy adulthood. Jesus never called us to make converts. He called us to make disciples, to bring them into the family where values can be imparted and character formed. What heartless human would birth a baby and leave it in the street?

I'm not indicting, blaming, or accusing those who minister out there in the public arena for not bringing people into the fold. It's not their fault. The problem I see is that the church has made a bad name for itself in the world. The bride of Christ should be glorious and beautiful, winsome and loving, but this is not the image we've presented to the world. Unfortunately, we have too often presented ourselves as judgmental and even hateful of those by whom we feel threatened—liberal politicians, homosexuals, illegal aliens, and so on. The list is long. Church has become the last place a person newly touched by the Spirit of the Lord would want to come, and yet the church remains at the very center of God's plan.

Two challenges therefore lie before us. The first is how to bridge the gap from the street or the marketplace into the company of the saints. The second has to do with cultivating the kingdom of God on earth, every church an outpost of heaven, an ambassadorial residence for our Savior and Lord where the laws of love, the principles of heaven, and the Father's heart prevail. This book is not the place to present the fullness of that vision. I've written others on that subject. In this setting, I merely issue the challenge. Do our fellowships reflect the prayer of Jesus that the Father's will be done on earth as it is in heaven? If not, why not, and if we truly desire for that to happen what must change? The stage has been set. The culture around us has shifted. The harvest is ripening.

CHAPTER 11

# THE FALL OF BABYLON AND THE RAPTURE OF THE CHURCH

REVELATION TELLS A STORY, NOT OF FEAR AND DOOM BUT of unfolding victory. "And another angel, a second one, followed, saying, 'Fallen, fallen is Babylon the great, she who has made all the nations drink of the wine of the passion of her immorality'" (Rev. 14:8). "For all the nations have drunk of the wine of the passion of her immorality, and the kings of the earth have committed acts of immorality with her, and the merchants of the earth have become rich by the wealth of her sensuality" (Rev. 18:3)

In 586 B.C., Babylon conquered Judah and Jerusalem, utterly destroyed both the city and the temple, and carried the cream of the population into seventy years of exile. For seventy years they languished under a regime that sought to erase their Jewish identity and pervert their faith by forcing the worship of Chaldean gods and even of the king himself. Thus, Babylon became a primary biblical paradigm for future oppressive and immoral societies opposed to God, His laws, and His principles.

Historically speaking, Babylon in Revelation symbolizes the Roman Empire of John's day, hundreds of years after the Babylonian exile, rife with immorality and viciously persecuting the church. In keeping with prophetic perspective, however, what John wrote foreshadows something larger yet to come.

The world, as we have known it, teeters on the brink of collapse. Even as people have become hungry for something transcendent, contemporary culture has evolved in a way that has become actively hostile toward those of us who stand on the Word of God and refuse to call evil good and good evil. With its promotion of lawlessness and sexual hedonism, the entertainment industry in the western world has polluted the whole earth and fed cultural deterioration in virtually every nation. Media conditions the way societies think, feel, and believe. Economically, the entire world depends on America for trade and prosperity, just as did the nations ruled over by the Roman Empire in John's day. Does this not sound very much like the description of Babylon the Great? It certainly reflects conditions in the Roman Empire at the time that John wrote and it points forward in time to the shape of world culture in our own day.

Even as many are being won to Jesus—or perhaps *because* so many are being won to Jesus—we have only just begun to see the hatred directed against Christians around the world. As we stand out for not going with the defiled cultural flow, multitudes will come to understand that the reason we refuse to go along is that we love God and that we know sin doesn't work. The brightness of our shining will highlight the misery of those who walk in darkness and a harvest of souls will result.

Regardless of how many turn to Jesus, however, the established culture of the west and other nations of the world will increasingly consider us to be a dangerous threat. Our worldview, our morals, and our dedication to God will be seen by the opposing culture as hatred for those whose lifestyles and philosophies we cannot approve of. It will seem to them incomprehensible that we could love and show grace and honor while not agreeing. We may see windows of favor and respite from this rising tide, but the overall trend will continue.

Currently, something like 100,000 Christians suffer martyrdom every year, but even that toll of precious lives reaps a harvest of victory. In November 2017 at the Global Prophetic Consultation in Dallas, Texas, I had the privilege of sharing dinner with a Christian leader from India, a nation ruled by Hindus. Repeatedly, he spoke of preaching to crowds of hundreds of thousands and of the resulting dramatic increase in souls being won in his nation. He attributed this to the blood of the martyrs crying out to God in a nation where churches are burned and Christians are killed. I say yet again that we get to win, even as darkness covers the earth!

God promises that this evil end-time culture, metaphorically named "Babylon" and foreshadowed in first- and second-century Rome, will fail and fall, just as both literal Babylon and Rome eventually did. In the early fourth century, Rome "fell" to the Christians, having been declared "Christian" by the emperor Constantine, although it never really reflected the character of the Lord whose name it claimed. It then crumbled as an empire. John foresaw something much wider and larger that would involve the entire world system in the last days.

## THE MESSAGE FOR BELIEVERS

Revelation contains a message of hope and reassurance of ultimate victory to believers under pressure. On God's timeline, final victory has been decreed and secured. To Him, it is already real. In light of this, John wrote to say that we must stand our ground and know that the difficult days of persecution and trial cannot last. The end has been determined in heaven and the outcome has been established in our favor.

### Idolatrous Worship

According to Revelation 14, the mark of the beast includes idolatrous worship in some form. In John's day, this included not only worship of the pantheon of Roman gods but worship of the Roman emperor. Emperor worship began with Augustus, the emperor who ruled during the time of Jesus's birth, as an outpouring of gratitude for the *Pax Romana*, the

Peace of Rome, that brought prosperity to the whole of the Mediterranean basin.

Before that century had ended, emperor worship had become a powerful movement. In some cities, Christians came under persecution for their refusal to sacrifice a pinch of incense to the emperor once a year while declaring, "Caesar is Lord." This could be seen as an act of rebellion and sedition against the state and was often dealt with as such. As noted earlier, the issue of buying and selling in John's prophecy had much to do with the requirement of belonging to a trade guild dedicated to one of the Roman gods in order to do business or practice a trade.

### Ownership or Service

Rather than think of a literal brand or mark of some kind, as we have examined in earlier sections, does it not make more sense to see the mark of the beast as symbolic of where one's loyalties lie? Remember the Roman practice of branding their slaves on the forehead to mark ownership? Whom then do we serve? What compromises are we willing to make with an ungodly and/or idolatrous system? Will we now water down or hide our commitment as Christians just so that we can get along in the world? Do we remain silent for fear of losing our jobs? And if we do keep silent, do we not sacrifice the lives and eternal destinies of those the Lord called us to reach?

Or will we drink of the strength and authority poured out on us through the Holy Spirit to rise above it all and minister the power of the kingdom of God? Will we adopt, not a siege mentality, but choose rather to believe the words of Jesus in Matthew 16:18, second half of the verse, "I will build My church; and the gates of Hades will not overpower it." Because of us, the structures of hell throughout the world are on the defensive. We win!

## Phylacteries Again

Once again, to review Chapter 4 of this book, the mark of the beast on the hand and forehead is a symbol drawn from Deuteronomy 6:6-8, not meant to be taken literally. This would have been easily understood by a Jewish audience in John's day.

> These words, which I am commanding you today, shall be on your heart. You shall teach them diligently to your sons and shall talk of them when you sit in your house and when you walk by the way and when you lie down and when you rise up. You shall bind them as a sign on your hand and they shall be as frontals on your forehead.

Thus, to this day the orthodox obey this command in literal fashion to mark their dedication to God, and to God alone. Anyone compromising with idolatry or submitting to the ungodly demands of an unholy culture, therefore, bears the mark of the beast.

"And the smoke of their torment goes up forever and ever; they have no rest day and night, those who worship the beast and his image, and whoever receives the mark of his name" (Rev. 14:11). Idolatrous compromise carries with it serious consequences! Those who belong to God dwell with Him in victory. Those who belong to the world system, the beast, go to hell. The threat of hell has become an unpopular doctrine in our day, but the warning stands. No amount of exegetical gymnastics can remove what is written or change its meaning.

# AT LAST! THE RAPTURE!

In Revelation 14:12, John drew a contrast between those who fall to compromise with idolatry and those who stand their ground under the pressure of an idolatrous and immoral culture in the period leading up to the Lord's return and the rapture of the church: "Here is the perseverance of the saints who keep the commandments of God and their faith in Jesus." By "here" he meant the period of time he previously described in which perseverance would be required.

Pressure requiring perseverance could go beyond economics to include suffering and death. Throughout history, this has, in fact, cost the lives of many who stood for the covenant. In many parts of the world, it continues to do so today, and it will again. Under societal pressure to compromise, to despair, to cave in, to live for self, we are called to stand our ground; and if we don't, we will be placing ourselves in real danger. For those who do stand, victory is assured.

> And I heard a voice from heaven, saying, "Write, 'Blessed are the dead who die in the Lord from now on!'" "Yes," says the Spirit, "so that they may rest from their labors, for their deeds follow with them" (Revelation 14:13).

The time comes when we must stand for the faith and for the Word once received, no matter what the price might be, and then know that we will reap the reward of the Lord's blessing.

## Rapture of the Righteous

"Then I looked, and behold, a white cloud, and sitting on the cloud was one like a son of man, having a golden crown on

His head and a sharp sickle in His hand" (Rev. 14:14). "One like a son of man" points to Jesus's own self-identification and is drawn from Daniel's vision in Daniel 7:13-14.

"And another angel came out of the temple, crying out with a loud voice to Him who sat on the cloud, 'Put in your sickle and reap, for the hour to reap has come, because the harvest of the earth is ripe'" (Rev. 14:15). The angel bears a message from the Father instructing Jesus to put in His sickle and reap. Here Jesus returns at last to gather us to Himself!

As Jesus Himself stated, at least in His earthly ministry, not even the Son knew the hour (see Matt. 24:36; Mark 13:32). Even now, risen, ascended, and sitting at the right of the Father in heaven, He waits to hear the Father's command. When the Father speaks that word of release, Jesus will come to gather His own. All of this parallels Matthew 24:29-31:

> But immediately after the tribulation of those days the sun will be darkened, and the moon will not give its light, and the stars will fall from the sky, and the powers of the heavens will be shaken. And then the sign of the Son of Man will appear in the sky, and then all the tribes of the earth will mourn, and they will see the Son of Man coming on the clouds of the sky with power and great glory. And He will send forth His angels with a great trumpet and they will gather together His elect from the four winds, from one end of the sky to the other.

"Then He who sat on the cloud swung His sickle over the earth, and the earth was reaped" (Rev. 14:16). Clearly and indisputably, what we call the rapture comes *after* the time when Christians will have been dying for their faith, *after* the Great Tribulation and the collapse of end-time Babylon, and just before Jesus brings this evil age to its ultimate end. It will come by the direct intervention of the Lord as He gathers His people to Himself.

### Harvest of the Wicked

As part of the same complex of events—notice that the context places these events in immediate proximity to one another—the wicked are harvested from the earth to a different destiny than the righteous, the 144,000 "sons of God." "And another angel came out of the temple which is in heaven, and he also had a sharp sickle" (Rev. 14:17). This angel stands ready to harvest the wicked of the earth.

> Then another angel, the one who has power over fire, came out from the altar; and he called with a loud voice to him who had the sharp sickle, saying, "Put in your sharp sickle and gather the clusters from the vine of the earth, because her grapes are ripe." So the angel swung his sickle to the earth and gathered the clusters from the vine of the earth, and threw them into the great wine press of the wrath of God. And the wine press was trodden outside the city, and blood came out from the wine press, up to the horses' bridles, for a distance of two hundred miles (Revelation 14:18-20).

John saw two back-to-back reapings almost as if they were one connected event unfolding in two parts. One harvest will include the "sons of God," the symbolic 144,000 fully dedicated believers who will be gathered in by Jesus Himself. The other reaping will gather those who do not belong to the Lord into the final expression of the Lord's wrath. All of this comes as one complex of end-time events that will unfold in the fullness of time. "The harvest is ripe." The victory is certain!

# CHAPTER 12

# SEVENTY WEEKS OF YEARS

*Then there was given me a measuring rod like a staff; and someone said, "Get up and measure the temple of God and the altar, and those who worship in it. Leave out the court which is outside the temple and do not measure it, for it has been given to the nations; and they will tread under foot the holy city for forty-two months."*

—REVELATION 11:1-2

155

F ORTY-TWO MONTHS—IN OTHER PLACES EXPRESSED AS A time, two times, and half a time; as 1,280 days; or as three and a half years—became a biblical paradigm or symbol for a period in which God's people suffer oppression and persecution. Historically, this is drawn from the days of Antiochus Epiphanes, the Greek who hideously and viciously conquered and oppressed Israel from 168 to 165 B.C.—approximately three and a half years. Passionate to spread and enforce his version of Greek culture, he outlawed the practice of Judaism on pain of death, erected an image of Zeus in the temple of the Lord, and sacrificed a pig on its altar.

Much later, after Jesus had been crucified and resurrected, and after Stephen the deacon had been stoned to death, a rebellion of the Jews broke out against Rome with a messianic pretender named Menachem exerting significant influence. The rebellion surfaced in A.D. 66 and ended with the utter and catastrophic destruction of Jerusalem in A.D. 70, approximately three and a half years after it began.

This is where the seventy weeks of years in Daniel come in.

> Seventy weeks have been decreed for your people
> and your holy city, to finish the transgression, to
> make an end of sin, to make atonement for iniquity,
> to bring in everlasting righteousness, to seal up
> vision and prophecy and to anoint the most holy
> place. So you are to know and discern that from the
> issuing of a decree to restore and rebuild Jerusalem
> until Messiah the Prince there will be seven weeks
> and sixty-two weeks; it will be built again, with
> plaza and moat, even in times of distress. Then
> after the sixty-two weeks the Messiah will be cut off

157

*and have nothing, and the people of the prince who is to come will destroy the city and the sanctuary. And its end will come with a flood; even to the end there will be war; desolations are determined. And he will make a firm covenant with the many for one week, but in the middle of the week he will put a stop to sacrifice and grain offering; and on the wing of abominations will come one who makes desolate, even until a complete destruction, one that is decreed, is poured out on the one who makes desolate* (Daniel 9:24-27).

The seventy weeks of years completes the prophecies of the coming of the Messiah and fulfills every prophecy concerning that manifestation of the nation-state of Israel in that particular expression of history. Sixty-nine weeks of years works out rather perfectly from the decree of Artaxerxes that the Jews could return to the land after the Babylonian exile, until the beginning of Jesus's ministry. Jesus ministered three and a half years before His perfect sacrifice on the cross put an end to sacrifices once and for all.

If we then suppose that perhaps three and a half more years passed until the stoning of Stephen the deacon, marking the formal rejection of Jesus by the Jewish nation, we have the completion of the seventy weeks of years, the fulfillment and sealing up of the prophecies applying to Israel up until the time of Jesus. Then in A.D. 70, the Romans utterly destroyed Jerusalem and decisively crushed the Jewish rebellion. Once again, therefore, we see this pattern of three and a half years repeated.

Much popular teaching separates the seventieth week out to the end time two millennia later. This is illegitimate use of Scripture. It imposes a supposition not intrinsic to the actual words used. Absent any textual indication that the seventieth week should be separate from the sixty-nine, accurate interpretation of Scripture in context requires that the seventy weeks be consecutive, thus ending in the ministry of Jesus and then the stoning of Stephen. Sacrifice ends in the middle of the seventieth week, three and a half years after the beginning of Jesus's ministry, not by decree of the antichrist as is so often taught, but rather because Jesus fulfilled the sacrificial system by becoming the final and complete sacrifice for sin. Satan was then defeated when Jesus rose from the dead, a victory that should inform our own lives and the manner in which we carry ourselves as believers.

Prophecies of the rebuilding of the temple in Jerusalem were fulfilled after the return from exile seventy years after the exile began. In light of an accurate interpretation of the seventy weeks of years and the end of sacrifice brought about by the crucifixion of Jesus, there remains no need to expect a third temple to be built as so many have assumed. As I have previously stated, a leading Jewish rabbi from the Los Angeles area was invited to address a class I took on Judaism and Christianity at Fuller Seminary in 1976. One of my fellow students asked about the rebuilding of the temple. The answer was, "No. We're not rebuilding the temple. We don't need a temple for sacrifice. We have repentance."

As for Jerusalem being trampled under foot by the Gentiles until the time of the Gentiles would be fulfilled (see Luke 21:24), consider this. From the time of the destruction of Jerusalem forward, the gospel went increasingly to the

Gentiles. Messianic congregations faded away until at last, in A.D. 325, the Council of Nicea expunged Jewish influence from the life of the church. Tragically, centuries of persecution of the Jews by the church ensued. Messianic congregations virtually ceased to exist, and the body of Christ lost the balance God had originally put in place. In this figurative sense, Jerusalem was trampled under foot by the Gentiles until the time of the Gentiles would be fulfilled.

I realize that many believe the current nation of Israel and the recovery of Jerusalem fulfills this prophecy concerning the dominance of the Gentiles coming to an end. Jerusalem was indeed held by Gentiles until the Six Day War in 1967 when the city was occupied once more by Israel. I would never minimize the significance of that event, nor would I deny that God had a hand in the victory, but I'm saying there may be more to it. As a sign of the end times, our victory, and the return of the Lord, the rise of the two witnesses in Revelation 11 may be more significant than the rebirth of the nation of Israel in 1948 or the recovery of Jerusalem by the Jews. Pay close attention to these things because I'm leading up to something important in the next chapter.

# CHAPTER 13

# THE TWO WITNESSES: A SIGN OF HOPE

MUCH HAS BEEN SAID AND WRITTEN CONCERNING THE two witnesses in Revelation 11:1-15. What I am about to present has the potential to be received either as significant revelation and a wonderful sign of the soon return of the Lord, or it will upset some and enrage others.

> *"And I will grant authority to my two witnesses, and they will prophesy for twelve hundred and sixty days, clothed in sackcloth." These are the two olive trees and the two lampstands that stand before the Lord of the earth* (Revelation 11:3-4).

Who are the two witnesses? Are they two individual people who will emerge at the end as most commentators would contend? Or are they something else?

The answer becomes clear in the words, "These are the two olive trees and the two lampstands that stand before the Lord of the earth." We must always interpret Scripture by Scripture, especially when symbols and explanations of their meaning occur within a single book of the Bible. Revelation 1:20 identifies lampstands as symbolic representations of churches, "the seven lampstands are the seven churches." Again in Revelation 2:5 John connected a lampstand with a church when he addressed the church in Ephesus. "Therefore remember from where you have fallen, and repent and do the deeds you did at first; or else I am coming to you and will remove your lampstand out of its place unless you repent."

If John established lampstands as symbolic representations of churches, then, interpreting Scripture by Scripture, we must understand the two witnesses not as individual men, but rather as two churches. We must therefore identify the two witnesses as two bodies of believers in Jesus. Revelation interprets Revelation.

What God revealed to John was His vision for two groups of believers, differentiated by heritage and culture, standing together, even in their different expressions, while reaching out to two culturally different groups of people. One was to be the Jewish wing of the church practicing a uniquely Jewish form of faith in Jesus. This would preserve Jewish culture and identity, as well as ensuring that knowledge of the Jewish roots of Christianity would not be forgotten. The other was to be the Gentile wing composed of non-Jews who had received Jesus. While these Gentile believers would not be Jewish in heritage, culture, or practice, they would be enriched by the knowledge of where their truth came from, as well as by the fellowship of their Jewish elder brothers and sisters in the faith.

In John's day, the two wings of the church existed side by side, composed of Jews who received Jesus as Messiah and Gentiles who believed. Historically, the Jewish expression of the church virtually passed out of existence in the years following the stoning of Stephen and the eventual destruction of Jerusalem. The Council of Nicea in A.D. 325 sealed it. "Jerusalem," figuratively and symbolically, was then trampled underfoot by the Gentiles as the Gentile expression of the church completely dominated the faith from approximately the second century until the present time.

In Romans 11, the apostle Paul wrote that before the end of it all, the Jews would be grafted back into the trunk from which they had been broken off. In fact, he spoke of the olive tree of Judaism springing forth from its roots in Abraham into which the Gentiles had been grafted and into which the

Jews who were broken off would once more be grafted and restored through faith in Jesus, their Messiah. We therefore have a dual symbolism in Revelation and in the Book of Romans confirming that the two witnesses must be the two expressions of Christianity restored to balance in the last days, identified both as an olive tree with native and wild branches and as lampstands.

According to the *Jewish Journal* in an article published in 2012, there were at that time 800 Messianic congregations in the world, "up from zero in 1967."[1] More have emerged since then. I have spoken with Messianic Jewish rabbis from Israel who testify to a significant increase in Messianic synagogues in Israel itself over the course of recent decades.

We are witnessing the restoration of the balance God intended from the very beginning of the church. This is a victorious sign of the approaching return of the Lord as these two witnesses, two wings of the church, begin to bear a more complete witness to the world than either could alone. More importantly, as opposed to the efforts of the church over the centuries to suppress Jewish heritage and expression, I see a tremendous increase today in interaction and love between Jews and Christians. In fact, significant numbers of churches now reach out even to Jewish non-believers for reconciliation and unity. Gentile churches increasingly work together with messianic Jewish congregations in demonstrations of oneness. We are looking at the development of a restored end-time body of Christ. Victory! Remember that this book presents an end-time word of hope!

As previously noted, drawn from actual historical events, forty-two months has long been the paradigm, the symbolic period of time, representing seasons when God's people suffered oppression and stood for their faith. This is drawn from 168-165 B.C. (three and a half years) when the Greek conqueror, Antiochus Epiphanes, occupied Judah and Jerusalem and viciously persecuted the Jews, defiled the temple, and destroyed anything that didn't reflect Greek culture. Later, from A.D. 66-70, a period of approximately three and a half years, the Jews engaged in rebellion against Rome until the Romans not only defeated the insurgents but destroyed Jerusalem and the temple at the cost of hundreds of thousands of lives. Believers in Jesus survived that holocaust to bear their witness.

Forty-two months can therefore be seen as symbolic of a period of time when the two witnesses will bear their testimony even under intense pressure and persecution. John foresaw a time of victory when the Jewish wing of the church would be revived and the people of God would once more enjoy the blessing of these two witnesses, together proclaiming the truth of Jesus as Son of God, Savior, and Messiah. Thus, we see messianic synagogues proliferating in our own day. The two witnesses now arise to bear their testimony with one voice in a troubled time—a certain sign of the soon return of the Lord.

"And if anyone wants to harm them, fire flows out of their mouth and devours their enemies" (Rev. 11:5). Expect that in the days leading to the Lord's return, the witness of the restored church will overcome the power of the world that comes against it. Consistently, the voice of God speaks through His prophets in the Word of God to promise victory in the last days.

Verses 7 and 8 speak of a time when the church in its two forms of witness will seem to have been destroyed or defeated. "When they have finished their testimony, the beast that comes up out of the abyss will make war with them, and overcome them and kill them" (Rev. 11:7).

The victory comes at Revelation 11:11. "But after the three and a half days, the breath of life from God came into them, and they stood on their feet; and great fear fell upon those who were watching them." The church cannot be stopped. The witness of Jesus cannot be silenced. Just as Jesus died and rose again, so the people of God in the form of the two witnesses—the two uniquely different expressions of the church—will appear to have been put down, only to rise once more in victory. Then, *after* this time of trouble, and when the victory has been won, the church will be caught up to heaven. "And they heard a loud voice from heaven saying to them, 'Come up here.' Then they went up into heaven in the cloud, and their enemies watched them" (Rev. 11:12).

Clearly, all of this happens while the church remains on earth in a period of tribulation. Consistently, God promises victory for the people of God in the last days and against all forms of opposition. It's not that we leave the earth in defeat. We don't leave the earth at all until we've decisively won.

To review, beginning at Revelation 11:5-6:

> *And if anyone wants to harm them, fire flows out of their mouth and devours their enemies; so if anyone wants to harm them, he must be killed in this way. These have the power to shut up the sky, so that rain will not fall during the days of their prophesying; and they have power over the waters to turn them into blood, and to strike the earth with every plague, as often as they desire.*

The symbolism here points to Moses and Elijah. The restored church in these latter days will experience an increase in authority, much like the authority Moses carried when he announced the plagues on Egypt that forced Pharaoh to release the people, and like that of Elijah who called for drought in Israel during the reign of Ahab in judgment for the worship of Baal.

The two witnesses therefore, Jewish and Gentile believers together, will minister freedom from bondage for God's people, and at the same time exercise power to break the strongholds of a godless culture fueled by the demonic influence of Baal. Through their witness, people will be set free from bondage, and the worship of demonic influences will be broken from them. None will be able to silence the voice of these end-time believers or blunt their influence as "fire flows out of their mouth and devours their enemies."

Persecution will arise at the end of this period. Opposition will seem to have defeated the church, but defeat will be neither the reality nor the final word. Revelation 11:7-8:

> *When they have finished their testimony, the beast that comes up out of the abyss will make war with them, and overcome them and kill them. And their dead bodies will lie in the street of the great city which mystically is called Sodom and Egypt, where also their Lord was crucified.*

There will come a time when the witness of the people of God will seem to have been permanently silenced.

*Those from the peoples and tribes and tongues and nations will look at their dead bodies for three and a half days, and will not permit their dead bodies to be laid in a tomb. And those who dwell on the earth will rejoice over them and celebrate; and they will send gifts to one another, because these two prophets tormented those who dwell on the earth. But after the three and a half days, the breath of life from God came into them, and they stood on their feet; and great fear fell upon those who were watching them. And they heard a loud voice from heaven saying to them, "Come up here." Then they went up into heaven in the cloud, and their enemies watched them. And in that hour there was a great earthquake, and a tenth of the city fell; seven thousand people were killed in the earthquake, and the rest were terrified and gave glory to the God of heaven. The second woe is past; behold, the third woe is coming quickly. Then the seventh angel sounded; and there were loud voices in heaven, saying, "The kingdom of the world has become the kingdom of our Lord and of His Christ; and He will reign forever and ever"* (Revelation 11:9-15).

In ancient times, to be left unburied in death constituted the ultimate dishonor. The church may appear to have been destroyed and discredited by the surrounding culture, but the voice of God's true people can never be silenced, even in martyrdom. The world may think it has "killed" the church, but even in what appears to be defeat, the world cannot hide or bury it. We will rise in a victory so complete as to ultimately destroy, dishonor, and shame the powers of darkness. Even today, many voices have declared the end of the institutional church, citing declining church attendance and the loss of a truly biblical worldview. Those who make these statements, however, fail to account for the rise of the 144,000 "sons of God" whose passion and fire even now grow ever brighter. The world may think it died, but the church will rise once more in power just before judgment falls. We get to win!

## NOTE

1.  an Jaben-Eilon, "Messianic Jewish Groups Claim Rapid Growth," Jewish Journal, June 12, 2012, http:// jewishjournal.com/culture/religion/105069.

# CHAPTER 14

# REVELATION 12: THE WOMAN CLOTHED WITH THE SUN

KEEP YOUR BIBLE OPEN AND HANDY BECAUSE AN ENTIRE chapter of Revelation is too much to quote on these pages.

People tend to lift out isolated verses to present the content of Revelation 12 as some kind of prehistoric expulsion of Satan and his angels from heaven. I propose a different view. Revelation 12 must be taken as one integrated story line, based in history, a heavenly or idealist representation of events on earth. Keep in mind that Revelation is both history that was relevant to those to whom John wrote in the first and second centuries, as well as containing prophetic foreshadowing of things to come.

Overall, Revelation presents the events of John's day while at the same time looking forward to things reserved for the last days. "The Revelation of Jesus Christ, which God gave Him to show to His bond-servants, the things which must soon take place; and He sent and communicated it by His angel to His bond-servant John" (Rev. 1:1). "Soon" must mean "soon"—not some primordial prehistoric past as viewed from our twenty-first century viewpoint.

## A BRIEF VIEW OF HISTORY

What, then, do the images related to the woman in Revelation 12 symbolically represent? Before I explain them, a quick summary of the underlying story may help. This chapter represents the history of the people of God who, in effect, collectively gave birth to Jesus the Messiah after centuries of gestation and preparation. As an infant, He escaped to Egypt after God warned His foster father, Joseph, that Herod wanted to kill Him. On earth, this was warfare, but a corresponding battle was fought in the heavens. Ultimately, in the ministry of

Jesus and His sacrifice, Satan was defeated by the blood of Jesus and was therefore denied access to heaven where his function had been to accuse the saints before the throne of God. See Job 1 as a reference.

Having failed to obliterate Jesus, and having been denied access to heaven, Satan then used the Roman Empire to pursue the church in an attempt to destroy it, but he failed once more. Before the Romans destroyed Jerusalem at the end of the Jewish rebellion, the Christians escaped to Pella, having been prophetically warned of what was to come. After that failure to snuff out the early church, the enemy of our soul went off to persecute and make war on believers in the rest of the Roman Empire.

When this history is overlaid on Revelation 12, it fits perfectly. Plainly stated, in Revelation 12 John saw actual history from a heavenly and spiritual perspective, looking back at it from his own time circa A.D. 90, twenty or so years after the destruction of Jerusalem. He understood the history of his people that prepared the way for Jesus. He knew, as well, what had happened to Jesus from birth to death and resurrection. He also knew what had happened with the messianic church in Jerusalem and what was currently coming against the Christians under the Roman Empire. It's all here.

## FIRST CENTURY JEWISH ASSUMPTIONS

In first-century Jewish thought, earthly and heavenly (spiritual) events are interrelated, with the heavenly either reflected in earthly events, or earthly events actually caused by heavenly ones.

References to the heavens in Scripture do not always mean "heavens" in the sense of God's paradise, but often refer to the spiritual realm in general. This is the case here in Revelation 12. For instance, Ephesians 6:12 refers to, "the spiritual forces of wickedness in the heavenly places." Clearly, the apostle Paul did not mean to say that wickedness exists in God's heaven. He wrote concerning the spiritual realm in general.

Earthly warfare, therefore, has a heavenly counterpart in the realm of the spirit. We battle here in the physical world while angels and demons engage in battle in the heavenly or spiritual realm. This can only be adequately represented symbolically.

# UNPACKING THE SYMBOLS

### *The Woman*

"A great sign appeared in heaven: a woman clothed with the sun, and the moon under her feet, and on her head a crown of twelve stars" (Rev. 12:1). In the ancient world surrounding Israel, these were common symbols associated with divinity. For Israel, however, this symbolism identifies the woman not as divine, but rather as supernatural in nature, a heavenly representation of something that is also earthly. Often, the prophets of the Old Testament referred to Israel as a woman. The twelve-starred crown identifies her as representing the people of Israel fathered by the twelve patriarchs. Verse 17 identifies the people of God on earth as her children, those begotten and born into the company of the people of God by faith, thus confirming the symbolic nature of the image.

Herein lies the element of hope and victory. The woman with the crown of twelve stars can be legitimately identified with the trunk of Israel in Romans 11, out of which grew

Jesus and into which we Gentiles have been grafted. Notice also the glory of the people of God. This woman, symbolic of the people of God, is clothed with the most brilliant light imaginable. The crown points to her status as royalty. Even under persecution, and even when faced with disfavor and governmental opposition, ultimate authority lies with God's people. We possess eternal royal status.

The woman represents both the people of Israel, whose history and heritage brought forth the Messiah, and literal Mary who gave birth to Jesus on earth. The fluidity of apocalyptic literature allows for this. It doesn't need to make logical sense any more than a dream must obey the rules of waking life. It's not as though John was thinking and reasoning through all of this and creating images out of his own head. He received the vision by the Holy Spirit in a trance state.

### The Dragon

"Then another sign appeared in heaven: and behold, a great red dragon having seven heads and ten horns, and on his heads were seven diadems" (Rev. 12:3). The color red symbolizes anger and war, while horns represent power. Seven is a number representing completion or fullness. Ten is another number of fullness. Both of these numbers, coupled with the diadems, indicate that in John's day Rome had complete sway.

Identifying the seven heads can be a bit problematic, possibly pointing to seven emperors or to the seven hills of Rome. In any case, the picture is of Rome, motivated by Satan, persecuting the church. Again, we see a heavenly counterpart to earthly events, not occurring in God's heaven but in the physical realm.

Drawn from Old Testament imagery, the dragon becomes the mythological embodiment of evil. Psalm 74:14 reads, "You crushed the heads of Leviathan; You gave him as food for the creatures of the wilderness." Later in Isaiah 27:1, "In that day the Lord will punish Leviathan the fleeing serpent, with His fierce and great and mighty sword, even Leviathan the twisted serpent; and He will kill the dragon who lives in the sea." And again, Isaiah 51:9, "Awake, awake, put on strength, O arm of the Lord; awake as in the days of old, the generations of long ago. Was it not You who cut Rahab in pieces, who pierced the dragon?"

Although verse 4 pictures his tail sweeping away a third of the stars of heaven to throw them to earth, in context we ought not to see this as the primordial fall of Satan from heaven. Why would Satan himself cast his own messengers out of heaven? Reliable scholars view it rather as a demonstration of the power of the dragon, symbolic of Rome. Rome, fueled and influenced by the devil, could be said to have ruled in power over a third of the known earth.

This being said, regardless of how you interpret these verses, at no point does Scripture present the dragon as ultimately victorious over God's people! We get to win!

### The Male Child

Verses 4 and 5 show us that in the fullness of time, Israel brought forth Jesus, the Messiah, King of Israel. "And she gave birth to a son, a male child, who is to rule all the nations with a rod of iron; and her child was caught up to God and to His throne" (Rev. 12:5). Dual symbolism could include a reference to Mary, His mother. The dragon sought Jesus's life as an infant but failed when Joseph heeded the angel and fled with mother and child to Egypt, and again when He was crucified, but He rose from the dead and ascended to heaven.

In verse 6, the woman flees to the wilderness for three and a half years where her life is preserved. Far from being a prophecy of the rapture of the saints, when the three and a half year Jewish rebellion broke out in A.D. 66, a prophetic warning led the Christians to escape to Pella prior to the siege of Jerusalem. Thus they avoided the destruction of the city.

Taken together, these verses and the symbolism embedded in them were, and are, intended to reassure believers at any point in history that the good plans of God will not be stopped, no matter how powerful the opposition. Set this against the current erosion of religious freedoms in the United States and other nations, as well as our growing fear of Islam, and what conclusion would you draw? God is good. God is love. He doesn't change. We therefore get to win! We live in hope, not in fear!

Verses 7-9 present a picture of Satan being thrown down with his "angels." The Greek word we translate "angels" does not always refer to powerful spiritual beings, much less powerful spiritual beings who fell from heaven. At root, it means merely "messengers." Satan and his messengers are denied any further access to heaven. The finished work of Jesus denied Satan any continuing right to approach the throne of God to accuse those who put their faith in Jesus. Verse 10 confirms this.

*Then I heard a loud voice in heaven, saying, "Now the salvation, and the power, and the kingdom of our God and the authority of His Christ have come, for the accuser of our brethren has been thrown down, he who accuses them before our God day and night."*

Much too often have we assigned more power and mystery to Satan and his messengers than is warranted.

Verse 12 calls for rejoicing over this victory. Ongoing persecution of Jesus's followers is prophesied in verse 13: "And when the dragon saw that he was thrown down to the earth, he persecuted the woman who gave birth to the male child." Again, in verse 14, you see the escape to Pella during the Jewish rebellion. That was the church in Jerusalem. Having failed to destroy the Jerusalem church, the dragon went off to pursue the Gentile church in the rest of the world:

*So the dragon was enraged with the woman, and went off to make war with the rest of her children, who keep the commandments of God and hold to the testimony of Jesus* (Revelation 12:17).

In the midst of it all, God empowers Christians to overcome. We have the assurance of ultimate victory.

# CHAPTER 15

# REVELATION 19 AND MORE: THE VICTORY

T HE CHAPTERS OF REVELATION PRECEDING CHAPTER 19 speak of the fall of the harlot beast of Babylon. In light of prophetic perspective, this was both Rome in the first centuries A.D. and a foreshadowing of the culture, society, and world order of the last days. While the early Christians needed to be reassured of ultimate victory in their day, so we take heart that the final and complete victory yet to come has been ordained in heaven, regardless of what we see in the world around us.

How do I know that Revelation 19 and the chapters to follow aren't limited to the first centuries? Rome, in fact, did not meet the kind of destruction described in Revelation. In reality, Christianity spread, the Christians effectively prevailed, and the empire began a transition under the emperor Constantine (A.D. 305-337) that culminated in him declaring the empire officially Christian. Eventually, Rome did fall, but not in the ways described in Revelation and not for some time after Constantine. Clearly, not everything prophesied by John came to pass in the early centuries. If we believe the Bible is true, then we look for more yet to come in a way that completely fulfills the word given.

"After these things," i.e. the great godless culture symbolized by Babylon, "I heard something like a loud voice of a great multitude in heaven, saying, 'Hallelujah! Salvation and glory and power belong to our God; because His judgments are true and righteous; for He has judged the great harlot who was corrupting the earth with her immorality, and He has avenged the blood of His bond-servants on her'" (Rev. 19:1-2). At the end of it all, the very angels of heaven rise up to say that at last the Lord has done it! It's over! Finally, God visits vengeance on those who have rejected Him, polluted His earth, and persecuted His people. Again, the victory!

# THE MARRIAGE SUPPER OF THE LAMB

At this point it becomes important to note that in Revelation the great marriage supper of the Lamb occurs not *before* the Great Tribulation, but rather *after* the victory of the believers who have come through it and *after* the destruction of godless end-time Babylon. This is so clearly stated in Revelation 19:6-9:

> *Then I heard something like the voice of a great multitude and like the sound of many waters and like the sound of mighty peals of thunder, saying, "Hallelujah! For the Lord our God, the Almighty, reigns. Let us rejoice and be glad and give the glory to Him, for the marriage of the Lamb has come and His bride has made herself ready." It was given to her to clothe herself in fine linen, bright and clean; for the fine linen is the righteous acts of the saints. Then he said to me, "Write, 'Blessed are those who are invited to the marriage supper of the Lamb.'" And he said to me, "These are true words of God."*

The contemporary church most often associates the wedding feast of the Lamb, as spoken of in Matthew 25, with the rapture.

> *Then the kingdom of heaven will be comparable to ten virgins, who took their lamps and went out to meet the bridegroom. Five of them were foolish, and five were prudent. For when the foolish took their lamps, they took no oil with them, but the prudent took oil in flasks along with their lamps. Now while*

*the bridegroom was delaying, they all got drowsy and began to sleep. But at midnight there was a shout, "Behold, the bridegroom! Come out to meet him." Then all those virgins rose and trimmed their lamps. The foolish said to the prudent, "Give us some of your oil, for our lamps are going out." But the prudent answered, "No, there will not be enough for us and you too; go instead to the dealers and buy some for yourselves." And while they were going away to make the purchase, the bridegroom came, and those who were ready went in with him to the wedding feast; and the door was shut. Later the other virgins also came, saying, "Lord, lord, open up for us." But he answered, "Truly I say to you, I do not know you"* (Matthew 25:1-12).

We are told to be ready, that like the bridegroom in the parable, the Lord could come at any time to rapture the church away. In the context of Jewish wedding customs in Bible times, however, "any time" was actually limited to any point in time within a clearly defined period of time. After approximately a year of betrothal, a ceremony would be held at which the groom would say to the bride, "I go to prepare a place for you. If I go and prepare a place for you, I will come again and receive you to Myself, that where I am, there you may be also." Jesus used these same words in John 14:2-3 as He prepared the disciples for His crucifixion, resurrection, and ascension into heaven—His going away and His ultimate return.

According to customs in Bible times, after making the statement Jesus quoted, the groom would then go to prepare the *chuppah*, the wedding chamber. Upon his return, he would attempt to surprise the bridal party by appearing at an unexpected hour at any time during a set period of time, generally not more than two weeks. That being said, the idea that Jesus could appear to rapture the church at any random point in history clearly doesn't work. We ought therefore to be able to identify a general period of time in which we might expect Him to return, but not the specific day or hour within that period of time.

Obviously, Revelation paints the picture of the marriage supper happening *after* the depredations of the great end-time culture of oppression and immorality have been judged and destroyed. The tribulation ends, and *then* the marriage supper is celebrated! We get to win, God sends His judgment upon the wicked, and *then* the Lord comes for His people!

Several terms describe those invited to the wedding feast. "Bond-servants" is the word employed in Revelation 19:2 and 5. Exodus 21:5-6 provides the background. "But if the slave plainly says, 'I love my master, my wife and my children; I will not go out as a free man,' then his master shall bring him to God, then he shall bring him to the door or the doorpost. And his master shall pierce his ear with an awl; and he shall serve him permanently" (Exod. 21:5-6). Having been freed from slavery by the blood of Jesus, those who love Him choose to surrender that freedom to become permanently devoted to Him in love.

More than merely bond-servants, the invitation includes those who have made themselves ready as a bride (see Rev. 19:7). This, however, refers not to individuals in isolation, but rather to the body of Christ collectively, implying relational connection in love, preparatory actions we must take to make ourselves ready, and a part we must decide to play. None of us can be the bride alone. Jesus will, "present to Himself the church in all her glory, having no spot or wrinkle or any such thing; but that she would be holy and blameless" (Eph. 5:27). The last days will be marked by a restored body of Christ, manifesting the kingdom of God on earth, cleansed and holy.

Finally, the invited company includes those who have sought and practiced righteousness (see Rev. 19:8). This takes us back to Romans 8:19, "For the anxious longing of the creation waits eagerly for the revealing of the sons of God," and Romans 8:29, "For those whom He foreknew, He also predestined to become conformed to the image of His Son, so that He would be the firstborn among many brethren." Those who have presumed upon cheap grace and neglected the pursuit of righteousness will find themselves left out. See Hebrews 12:14: "Pursue peace with all men, and the sanctification without which no one will see the Lord." *Sanctification* is the word for holiness that radiates from within and changes outward behavior. It's not about changing outward behavior in order to change the heart. The former is transformation by grace. The latter is legalism and life under the law.

## THE CONQUERING KING

*And I saw heaven opened, and behold, a white horse, and He who sat on it is called Faithful and True, and in righteousness He judges and wages war. His eyes are a flame of fire, and on His head are many diadems; and He has a name written on Him which no one knows except Himself. He is clothed with a robe dipped in blood, and His name is called The Word of God (Revelation 19:11-13).*

The primary purpose of the Book of Revelation is stated in the very first verse: "The Revelation of Jesus Christ, which God gave Him to show to His bond-servants, the things which must soon take place." The declared purpose of Revelation therefore comes in two parts. The first is to reveal the true nature of Jesus in the light of the second purpose, which is to show the first- and second-century church what must soon take place, things that would affect their lives. Remember that Revelation is rooted in history. It was addressed to seven real churches facing real situations. It includes end-time predictions but spoke as well to events in the first century.

We've rightly known Jesus as the Suffering Servant and Savior. Revelation now reveals Him as the conquering Messiah, Lord of the universe in all His glory. As I have said so many times, the story of the last days and the return of Jesus is a story of hope and victory.

### The White Horse

Biblically, horses symbolize power, while the color white indicates purity and holiness. In Revelation 19:11-13, Jesus is no longer the Suffering Servant or even the ascended Lord who was physically absent for millennia. Here He returns in the fullness of power, radiating the purity of His nature in love, morality, glory, and might.

### Faithful and True

Never abandoning, never breaking His promise, never speaking a lie, absolutely consistent, Jesus never changes. In the culture of Bible times, what is true is something reliable. He keeps His covenant. Having promised a return in glory and victory, He keeps His word.

### *Jesus as Judge*

Although we often define judgment as punishment, the root meaning in the original language of the Bible is to cut or separate. Jesus separates the precious from the vile, determining what has value, as opposed to that which does not. The end times and the coming of our Lord in victory are about the final separation of what is unholy and defiled from what is good and pure. In the present age, evil continues to produce evil, even while good produces good. While we can lament the polarizing of society as the forces of good and evil stand off against one another, we must also recognize this as the inevitable consequence of the division between those who press in passionately for holiness and those who move in the other direction. When Jesus returns, He will sort one from the other.

### *Jesus Wages War*

In order to destroy evil and establish justice, Jesus rides in holy wrath. We make a tragic mistake if we allow the gospel of grace to cause us to forget the wrath of God. Wickedness offends Him and provokes His rage. Jesus makes war on that which is not holy. His wrath actually expresses His love. Sin harms those whom He loves and He therefore moves to destroy it. When mankind has been given every chance to change direction and avail themselves of the salvation bought by His death and resurrection, Jesus must at last come to destroy evil and execute victory. To do less would not be love. Evil destroys. Love edifies and restores. To allow evil to exist in the kingdom of God would be to re-create the very evil Jesus came to conquer. It would make heaven into hell. Such would be neither kindness nor love. In the age to come, love, and love alone, prevails. We do get to win!

### Diadems and Other Symbols

*Diadems:* A diadem is a crown, representing Jesus's absolute lordship over heaven and over every nation on earth. Wearing multiple crowns, Jesus reveals Himself as Lord and King over every tribe, tongue, and nation. As absolute sovereign, He cannot be defeated. As His kids, neither can we. Victory!

*Eyes a flame of fire:* Fire purifies and consumes. Jesus's gaze penetrates, exposes, and consumes that which is unholy. No matter what lies, distortions, or delusions the enemy of our soul seeks to hide, Jesus will find it out, reveal it, and consume it to ash.

*The name no one knows.* In Hebrew tradition, the name of a thing represents the nature of that thing. Every name Jesus bears, therefore, expresses some aspect of His nature. The name *Jesus,* for instance, comes from the Hebrew *Yeshua,* which means "Yahweh saves." In this chapter of Revelation, we read that the human mind could not possibly grasp the depth of Jesus's true nature. He cannot be reduced to human understanding. Our concept of mercy could never match His. His mercy is infinite and we are finite. He is uncreated and we are the creatures. He is part of a Trinity, the Three who are One, a mystery we can never fathom. His very nature is eternal, outside of time. We have no way of grasping the fullness of that wonder. No name on the human tongue could possibly express the depth and mystery of who He is.

*Robe dipped in blood.* Battle in the Ancient Near East was a much bloodier affair than we often see today. Hand to hand combat and sword against sword meant that every warrior would be spattered, even drenched, in blood. In victory, Jesus will symbolically bear the blood from the battle He has fought and from the cross He has embraced in winning it.

*The Word of God.* Jesus is the perfect embodiment of God's total redemptive plan. Every part of Him, every action and word, expresses the nature of Father God and accomplishes His purposes.

## The Heavenly Army

"And the armies which are in heaven, clothed in fine linen, white and clean, were following Him on white horses" (Rev. 19:14). On earth Jesus became the Redeemer. At the end, He fully manifests as the victorious conqueror leading a heavenly army to put an end to evil and visit wrath upon it, all for the sake of the chosen whom He loves.

As prophesied in the gospels and other passages of the New Testament, this is an army of angels.

> *For whoever is ashamed of Me and My words in this adulterous and sinful generation, the Son of Man will also be ashamed of him when He comes in the glory of His Father with the holy angels* (Mark 8:38).

> *For whoever is ashamed of Me and My words, the Son of Man will be ashamed of him when He comes in His glory, and the glory of the Father and of the holy angels* (Luke 9:26).

> *For after all it is only just for God to repay with affliction those who afflict you, and to give relief*

*to you who are afflicted and to us as well when the Lord Jesus will be revealed from heaven with His mighty angels in flaming fire, dealing out retribution to those who do not know God and to those who do not obey the gospel of our Lord Jesus. These will pay the penalty of eternal destruction, away from the presence of the Lord and from the glory of His power, when He comes to be glorified in His saints on that day, and to be marveled at among all who have believed—for our testimony to you was believed* (2 Thessalonians 1:6-10).

Note that, while the army in this chapter accompanies Him, it doesn't fight because it doesn't need to. Jesus's mouth, His words, carry the day. He only needs to speak, even as He spoke at creation when the universe leaped into being at the sound of His voice. The battle therefore ends before it can even begin.

*From His mouth comes a sharp sword, so that with it He may strike down the nations, and He will rule them with a rod of iron; and He treads the wine press of the fierce wrath of God, the Almighty. And on His robe and on His thigh He has a name written, "KING OF KINGS, AND LORD OF LORDS"* (Revelation 19:15-16).

Some believe that Jesus ruling the nations with a rod of iron is the beginning of Jesus's millennial reign on earth, but this implies no such period of time. Jesus rules on earth by invitation, not by force. At the end, He comes to reign by defeating and destroying that which is evil, His only weapon being the sword from His mouth, His word. He will gain the victory and destroy wickedness, loosing wrath upon it simply by speaking.

### The Final Victory

> *Then I saw an angel standing in the sun, and he cried out with a loud voice, saying to all the birds which fly in midheaven, "Come, assemble for the great supper of God, so that you may eat the flesh of kings and the flesh of commanders and the flesh of mighty men and the flesh of horses and of those who sit on them and the flesh of all men, both free men and slaves, and small and great"* (Revelation 19:17-18).

Ancient warfare afforded no honor to the defeated. In fact, to be left unburied when slain in battle was seen as the ultimate state of dishonor. Enemy casualties would therefore often be left for the carrion birds to feast upon. The symbolism of this passage points to the devastating magnitude and finality of the victory. The statement that no one remains to bury the dead among the armies opposing the Lord indicates total destruction and utter humiliation for the enemy of our soul. That which once exalted itself in pride and power lies now shamed and abased on the field of battle. The victory is absolute and complete.

"And I saw the beast and the kings of the earth and their armies assembled to make war against Him who sat on the horse and against His army" (Rev. 19:19). In its historical context, John saw the Roman system of religion and government, the culture of figurative Babylon. First-century people living under Roman domination thought of the empire as the whole earth because Rome had conquered and ruled everything worth conquering and ruling over. In many nations, Rome allowed some measure of self-government under whatever kings the Romans suffered to remain. Thus, in John's day, all "the kings of the earth" stood opposed to the followers of Jesus.

In prophetic perspective, Rome foreshadowed the end-time world system that increasingly stands against Christianity today. To attack Jesus's people is to attack Jesus, just as Jesus said to Saul who became Paul, "Saul, Saul, why are you persecuting Me?" when on his way to attack and arrest followers of Jesus (Acts 9:4). When the world system attacks Christianity, and when Christians are persecuted and killed, Jesus takes it very personally.

Never should we see any of this turmoil and opposition against believers as a cause for fear. We get to win, remember? Jesus intervenes.

> *And the beast was seized, and with him the false prophet who performed the signs in his presence, by which he deceived those who had received the mark of the beast and those who worshiped his image; these two were thrown alive into the lake of fire which burns with brimstone* (Revelation 19:20).

What masqueraded as God by supernatural demonstration, real or counterfeit, is shown not to be God at all. Final destination? The lake of fire. No Roman emperor ever performed supernatural signs. In the mystery of prophetic perspective, here is the foreshadowing of the future end time.

The last-days culture of idolatry and hostility to Christian faith that was foreshadowed in Rome in John's day will manifest in fullness in the last days and come to a final end at the word of the Lord. "And the rest were killed with the sword which came from the mouth of Him who sat on the horse, and all the birds were filled with their flesh" (Rev. 19:21). Devastating defeat for the powers of darkness! Resounding victory for the saints!

As the culture of Babylon falls into rubble, the world, inspired by the devil, rises in wrath to oppose Jesus rather than recognize the truth and choose to repent. So, there will be one final demonic onslaught quickly ended by the word of Jesus's mouth. What follows will be the kingdom of God on earth in fullness. The old evil age will end that has existed alongside the kingdom of God as it came to earth in Jesus. Only the kingdom of God in all its purity will remain and we will all be changed in the twinkling of an eye at the last trumpet. As the apostle Paul wrote:

*Behold, I tell you a mystery; we will not all sleep, but we will all be changed, in a moment, in the twinkling of an eye, at the last trumpet; for the trumpet will sound, and the dead will be raised imperishable, and we will be changed* (1 Corinthians 15:51-52).

*For if we believe that Jesus died and rose again, even so God will bring with Him those who have fallen asleep in Jesus. For this we say to you by the word of the Lord, that we who are alive and remain until the coming of the Lord, will not precede those who have fallen asleep. For the Lord Himself will descend from heaven with a shout, with the voice of the archangel and with the trumpet of God, and the dead in Christ will rise first. Then we who are alive and remain will be caught up together with them in the clouds to meet the Lord in the air, and so we shall always be with the Lord. Therefore comfort one another with these words* (1 Thessalonians 4:14-18).

Couple First Thessalonians with the promise that we will inherit the earth and that the righteous will be put in charge of all that is the Lord's when the wicked are taken out, and you get the picture. Jesus returns, harvests the wicked from the earth, and catches us up to Himself where we join those who have died before and who come with Him at His return. We are changed in that moment. Then, in the same cataclysmic event, He creates a new heaven and a new earth on which we get to reign with Him eternally (see Rev. 21:1). In this picture, at best the rapture is a momentary and transitory thing while the earth is renewed by the word of the Lord before we, who have by now been changed, assume our inheritance upon it.

As Revelation 21 continues, God lives among us, the redeemed, on this new earth, in uninterrupted union. All suffering is eliminated and we live without death, illness, or decay. "He who overcomes will inherit these things, and I will be his God and he will be My son" (Rev. 21:7). It reads, "He who overcomes," not, "He who escapes." In order to inherit these things, the Revelation calls us to persevere, to overcome every obstacle, promising us power to do it and power to prevail. We walk in victory and then gloriously inherit the redeemed earth. *We get to win!*

# IN CLOSING

I FULLY REALIZE THAT I HAVE NOT ANSWERED ALL THE questions surrounding the return of the Lord and our ultimate victory. Many aspects of this wondrous sequence of events simply cannot be packaged in a nice, neat box. Some will never be understood this side of the Lord's return. Mystery remains. It does seem clear, however, that the thrust of Scripture assures victory for the people of God, both now in this age and in the age to come. As we stand in righteousness and persevere in devotion, then even in the midst of gathering darkness we shine brightly, reaping a harvest of souls, influencing and affecting every tribe, tongue, and nation.

Pretribulation rapture theory has no solid basis in Scripture and amounts to a defeatist theology in which we need to be rescued from a deteriorating world. It robs our children of the three-generational vision God has mandated and the destiny He has appointed for them. We cannot hold to an escapist/defeatist stance and, at the same time, preach a victorious gospel in keeping with the resurrection.

So, I finish where I began Chapter 2:

> *Arise, shine; for your light has come, and the glory of the Lord has risen upon you. For behold, darkness will cover the earth and deep darkness the peoples; but the Lord will rise upon you and His glory will appear upon you. Nations will come to your light, and kings to the brightness of your rising. Lift up your eyes round about and see; they all gather together, they come to you. Your sons will come from afar, and your daughters will be carried in the arms* (Isaiah 60:1-4).

# ABOUT
# R. LOREN SANDFORD

R. Loren Sandford has been in full-time ministry since 1976 and is a long-time international leader in renewal, as well as a prophetic voice. He is the founding pastor of New Song Church and Ministries in Denver, Colorado where he continues to serve, travels and teaches internationally, and has authored a number of books.

www.rlorensandford.com

OTHER BOOKS BY R. LOREN SANDFORD

*The Micaiah Company*

*Yes There's More*

*Visions of the Coming Days*

*Renewal for the Wounded Warrior*

*Understanding Prophetic People*

*Purifying the Prophetic*

*Wielding the Power to Change Your World*

www.ingramcontent.com/pod-product-compliance
Lightning Source LLC
Chambersburg PA
CBHW060756100426
42813CB00004B/845

* 9 7 8 0 7 6 8 4 4 5 6 9 5 *